Arbeitsblätter

Reading and writing skills
9./10. Schuljahr

24 Arbeitsblätter
mit didaktisch-methodischen Kommentaren

Sekundarstufe I

von Detlef und Margaret von Ziegésar

Ernst Klett Verlag
Stuttgart Düsseldorf Leipzig

Der Verlag hat sich nach bestem Wissen und Gewissen bemüht, alle Inhaber von Urheberrechten an Texten und Abbildungen zu diesem Werk ausfindig zu machen. Sollte das in irgendeinem Fall nicht korrekt geschehen sein, bitten wir um Entschuldigung und bieten an, gegebenenfalls in einer nachfolgenden Auflage einen korrigierten Quellennachweis zu bringen.

Bildquellennachweis:

S. 8: mev, GettyOne, Corel Corporation; **S. 9:** mev; **S. 10 l.:** AKG, Berlin; **S. 10 r.:** Jochen Tack, Das Fotoarchiv Essen; **S. 15:** © 1976 by Erco Leuchten GmbH; **S. 17:** www.canada.gc.ca/canadiana/lmap_e.html © 2001. Her Majesty the Queen in Right of Canada, Natural Resources Canada; **S. 18:** mev; **S. 22 l.:** mev; **S. 22 r.o.:** Michael Coyne, Das Fotoarchiv Essen; **S. 22 r.u.:** mev; **S. 25:** mev; **S. 26:** mev; **S. 28 o.:** © Bob Krist/Corbis/Picture Press Life; **S. 46/47:** The Works of Lewis Carroll/Illustrations: John Tenniel. Paul Hamlyn, London 1965, p. 66; **S. 50:** James Thurber: The rabbits who caused all the trouble. From: *Fables for our time* by James Thurber (Hamish Hamilton, 1939). Copyright © James Thurber, 1951; **S. 53:** mev

Die Deutsche Bibliothek – CIP-Einheitsaufnahme
Ein Titeldatensatz für diese Publikation ist bei
Der Deutschen Bibliothek erhältlich.

Auflage 5. 4. 3. 2. | 2006 2005 2004 2003
Alle Rechte vorbehalten
© Ernst Klett Verlag GmbH, Stuttgart 2002
Internetadresse: http://www.klett-verlag.de
E-Mail: klett-kundenservice@klett-mail.de
Umschlaggestaltung: BSS Werbeagentur Sachse und Partner, Bietigheim
Zeichnungen auf S. 12 (Abb. F, I), 24, 30, 33, 37, 44: Andreas Florian, Lübeck
DTP: Klaus Bauer, Bondorf
Druck und Bindung: Gutmann + Co. GmbH, 74388 Talheim. Printed in Germany.
ISBN 3-12-927819-2

Vorwort 4

Different ways of reading; text types
A 1: Reading habits 6
A 2: Recognising different types of texts 7

Skimming
A 3: Skimming advertisements / making telephone enquiries 8
A 4: Skimming with the help of illustrations and headings / making notes (table) 10
A 5: Reading and writing book descriptions ('blurbs') 12

Scanning for specific information
A 6: Scanning an advertisement / explaining (sports) rules in writing 14
A 7: Scanning an encyclopedia article / making notes (list) 16

Writing letters
A 8: Writing informal letters 18
A 9: Writing formal letters: applying for jobs 20

Reading for detail
A 10: An informative text / reorganising information 22
A 11: Conventional features of instructional texts / writing instructions 24
A 12: Identifying the main ideas in a newspaper article / linking ideas 26

Presenting arguments
A 13: Argumentative text / writing a balanced argument 28
A 14: Oral presentation of written texts / making notes, summarising ... 30
A 15: Debating / writing a poem 32

Summarising
A 16: Understanding an explanatory text / summarising non-fiction 35
A 17: Understanding a literary text / summarising fiction 37

Approaching literature
A 18: Understanding descriptive techniques / describing physical appearance 40
A 19: Direct and indirect characterisation / continuing a story 42
A 20: Characterisation through dialogue / writing dialogue 44

Humour and irony
A 21: Humour through taking things literally 46
A 22: Humorous poems: nonsense, puns / writing poetry 48
A 23: Irony and euphemisms in a fable 50

Creative reading and writing
A 24: Writing the ending to a short story / changing the point of view 52

Teaching notes 55

Index of text types and reading and writing skills 88

Vorwort

Allgemeines

Reading and writing skills 9./10. Schuljahr dient der systematischen Förderung des Leseverstehens und der schriftlichen Kompetenz im Englischunterricht der Sekundarstufe I. Ein Heft für die Klassen 7 und 8 liegt ebenfalls vor. Der erste Teil der einzelnen Bände enthält fotokopierbare Arbeitsblätter, deren Ausgangspunkt eine reiche Palette an verschiedenen authentischen Textsorten darstellt. Der zweite Teil besteht aus einem ausführlichen Lehrerkommentar mit detaillierten Hinweisen zum Einsatz der Arbeitsblätter im Unterricht samt Lösungsvorschlägen.

Typografisch hervorgehobene Tipps vermitteln den Schülern und Schülerinnen Lese- und Schreibstrategien und machen ihnen den Leseverstehens- und Schreibprozess bewusst. Drei das Inhaltsverzeichnis ergänzende Sachregister am Ende des Bandes listen die verwendeten Textsorten *(Type of text)* und die zur Übung anstehenden Lese- und Schreibfertigkeiten *(Reading skills, Writing skills)* auf. Dies ermöglicht den Lehrern und Lehrerinnen den gezielten Zugriff auf die verschiedenen Leseweisen, Schreibanlässe, Textsorten und Lese- und Schreibfertigkeiten.

Man kann die Arbeitsblätter in der vorgegebenen Reihenfolge kursmäßig durchnehmen, aber auch je nach Bedarf einzelne Arbeitsblätter zum gezielten Üben spezifischer Leseweisen oder bestimmter Schreibstrategien herausgreifen.

Leseverstehen

Die jüngste fremdsprachliche Leseforschung definiert Lesen als eine auf dem Zusammenspiel zweier Prozesse beruhende aktive Bedeutungskonstruktion. Zum einen geht die Sinnentnahme von den grafischen Daten des Textes aus (sog. *bottom-up*-Prozess), zum anderen bringt der Leser ein Vorwissen über den im Text behandelten Gegenstand mit. Dieses vom Leser an den Text herangetragene Vor- und Weltwissen baut eine jeweils individuelle Leseerwartung von oben her – *top-down* – auf, was zu einem das Verstehen fördernden ständigen Prozess des Erstellens von Hypothesen oder Inferenzen über den Text führt.

Gute Leser zeichnen sich dadurch aus, dass sie ihr generelles Weltwissen aktivieren und einbeziehen, während schlechte Leser häufig buchstäblich am Text „kleben" und mühsam Wort für Wort den Sinn zu erschließen suchen. Entscheidend für eine gezielte Leseförderung, wie sie die vorliegenden Arbeitsblätter anstreben, ist deshalb, beide Teilprozesse zu üben. Ein auf diesem interaktiven Modell des Leseverstehens basierendes reibungsloses Zusammenspiel beider Teilprozesse wird durch folgende, den Arbeitsblättern zugrunde gelegten Lernziele angestrebt:

1. Das Bewusstsein, dass es verschiedene *Leseabsichten* und verschiedene *Textsorten* gibt und dass je nach Leseabsicht eine bestimmte Textsorte ausgewählt wird (A 1, A 2).
2. Verschiedene Leseabsichten lassen sich am besten durch bestimmte erlernbare *Leseweisen* verwirklichen:
2.1. Beim *kursorischen* Lesen *(skimming)* versucht der Leser, zum Zwecke des globalen Verstehens einen ersten Überblick über den Text zu gewinnen (A 3 – A 5).
2.2. Beim *selektiven* Lesen *(scanning)* wird ein Text so lange rasch überflogen, bis man eine gesuchte Information gefunden hat (A 6 – A 7).
2.3. Beim *intensiven* Lesen *(reading for detail)* sollen Textinhalt und Intention des Autors möglichst vollständig und differenziert erfasst werden. Das intensive Lesen kommt zum Einsatz bei bestimmten Sachtexten (A 10 – A 12), beim Interpretieren literarischer Texte (A 17 – A 24) und beim *creative reading* literarischer Texte, wenn der Leser z. B. eine Geschichte zu Ende schreiben oder einen Perspektivwechsel vornehmen soll (A 24).
3. Die Schüler und Schülerinnen lernen, dass sie durch den Einsatz ihres Vor- und Weltwissens einen Text besser verstehen können. Diese Vorkenntnisse werden, wenn erforderlich, in den Arbeitsblättern durch geeignete *Pre-reading*-Aufgaben aktiviert.

Schreiben

Den von der modernen Schreiblehrforschung formulierten Lernzielen folgend, sollen die Schüler und Schülerinnen lernen, dass der Autor eines Textes eine bestimmte *Schreibabsicht* verfolgt, zwischen verschiedenen *Textsorten* mit ihren *spezifischen Merkmalen* wählen kann und sowohl die sprachlichen und textuellen *Vorkenntnisse* als auch das *Weltwissen* seiner Adressaten berücksichtigen muss.

Dieses Textbewusstsein gewinnen die Lernenden bei den auf die Lesephase folgenden textverarbeitenden Lerngesprächen und den sich daran anschließenden, *post-reading activities* darstellenden Schreibaufgaben, die sich von stark gelenkten zu offenen Aufgabentypen bewegen. Den gelenkten Schreibaufgaben dienen die vorangestellten Lesetexte als sprachliches und inhaltliches Modell, und die Lernenden üben, die den verschiedenen Textsorten zugrunde liegenden Textnormen zu erfüllen (A 5, A 6, A 8, A 9, A 11 – A 13, A 16). Die offeneren Aufgabentypen fordern von den Lernenden selbstständig zu erbringende sprachliche und gedankliche Leistungen im Sinne des kreativen Schreibens (A 15, A 20, A 22, A 24).

Zur Gewinn bringenden Verarbeitung des Gelesenen üben die Lernenden mehrere Arbeitstechniken ein: Verschiedene Typen von Notizen – *making notes* in Form von Tabellen, Listen oder *mind maps* – dienen dem systematischen Ordnen des Gelesenen sowie der Informationsreduzierung und -speicherung (A 4, A 7, A 16). *Summaries* eignen sich sowohl als Erinnerungshilfe als auch zur schnellen Informationswiedergabe (A 14, A 16, A 17).

Sprechen

Die mündliche Kompetenz der Schüler und Schülerinnen wird in den auf die Lesetexte und die von den Lernenden selbst verfassten Texte folgenden Lerngesprächen gefördert sowie in zwei, sich der Kommunikationsform *debating* (A 15) und der Technik der Präsentation (A 13 – A 14) widmenden gesonderten Arbeitsblättern.

A1 Reading habits

1. Your attitudes to reading

Do you read a lot in your own language? What kind of things do you read? This questionnaire will help you to think about your attitude to reading.

1. When did you last read a book?
   a) I can't remember .... ❏
   b) Sometime in the last month............. ❏
   c) Last week .... ❏

2. What was it about?
   a) I can't remember .... ❏
   b) I have a vague idea.................. ❏
   c) I could tell you all about it .... ❏

3. Who wrote it?
   a) I don't know..................... ❏
   b) I can't remember .... ❏
   c) I know........................ ❏

4. Why did you read it?
   a) I had to read it for school .... ❏
   b) Someone gave it to me .... ❏
   c) I wanted to .... ❏

5. Did you enjoy it?
   a) No, it was terrible.................. ❏
   b) It was all right .... ❏
   c) Yes, it was good................... ❏

6. Do you have a favourite author?
   a) No. I only read what I have to........... ❏
   b) No, I like lots of different ones........... ❏
   c) Yes.......................... ❏

7. How many books do you own?
   a) One or two...................... ❏
   b) At least eight .... ❏
   c) More than twelve .... ❏

8. If someone gave you a book token* would you
   a) give it away or sell it?............... ❏
   b) have a rough idea of what you might buy?... ❏
   c) buy a book you want?............... ❏

9. What about newspapers and magazines? Do you
   a) just look at the pictures?.............. ❏
   b) skim through them and read anything
      that looks interesting? .... ❏
   c) start at the beginning and go right through
      them?........................ ❏

10. Do you do any reading for school?
    a) No, not if I don't have to .... ❏
    b) Yes, if the subject interests me .... ❏
    c) I try to find more information
       so that I will get better marks .... ❏

11. Have you ever been to your local library?
    a) No, never .... ❏
    b) Yes, about a year ago .... ❏
    c) Yes, a few weeks ago .... ❏

➡ **Let's see how you got on:**

If most of your answers were (a)s you don't seem to enjoy reading much. Maybe you haven't found anything that interests you yet? Try something different.

Mostly (b)s: Could it be that you're a bit lazy? Why not ask other people if they know some really good stories?

Mostly (c)s: You enjoy reading. Don't always choose the same type of thing, though. Try lots of different types of books.

Vocabulary: *book token* – card, usually given as a present, which can be exchanged for a book in a shop

2. The things you read

Think about the kinds of books you have read in the last few months. Can you remember where you got them from?

For example: *Thrillers – from the library*

3. My choice

Think of one of your favourite books. Write a few sentences explaining what it is about and why you think your classmates would enjoy it.

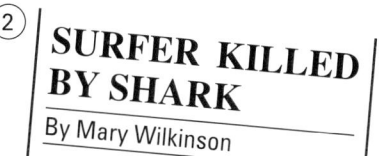

Recognising different types of texts — A2

1. Recognising different kinds of writing

Look at all these different kinds of writing. If you are a good reader you will immediately recognise what type of texts they are. Match them with the descriptions.

○ Newspaper article ○ Public notice
○ Letter to a magazine ○ Postcard ○ Instructions
○ Message or note ○ Formal letter ○ Advertisement
○ Novel ○ Diary ○ Film review

TIP: When you start reading anything make sure you know what type of text it is.

1. Ring Mum at six

2. SURFER KILLED BY SHARK
By Mary Wilkinson
A teenage surfer was killed yesterday when he …

3. "I have the Nokia Communicator so I can communicate any way I like. I make a lot of calls, of course. …"

4. played the same trick last week and made a fool of me. What shall I do?
(Chris, 15, Brighton)
☞ Stop listening to your friends and listen to yourself. Try to …

5. OPENING HOURS
MON. 10.00 – 6.00
TUES. 10.00 – 5.30

6. Spent all day on beach yesterday. Home again on Saturday. See you soon.

7. I would be grateful if you could send me some information about

8. KEEP TO THE LEFT
SIGNAL LEFT when you want to leave a roundabout

9. Michael Almereyda's **Hamlet**
Shakespeare's classic drama is set in modern New York. Hamlet, a filmmaker, returns home when his father dies.

10. I lay awake. Wondering what the next day would be like.

11. Letter from college, interview next Thursday.

A3 Skimming advertisements / making telephone enquiries

1. Looking through advertisements

Look at all these advertisements. Without reading them in detail run your eye over them quickly – 'skim' through them – so that you know roughly what they are about.

1. What are the advertisements for?
2. Cover the advertisements up and try to remember some of the different types of holidays.
3. Pick out two adverts which would interest you and explain why.
4. Which advert does not interest you at all? Why not?

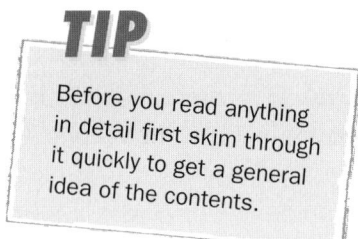

TIP

Before you read anything in detail first skim through it quickly to get a general idea of the contents.

Sherpa Expeditions
Worldwide walking and trekking holidays
Anything from a gentle walk in Tuscany to a Himalayan expedition.
Call 020 8577 7187

UK HOLIDAYS
CANAL BOATING
... Relaxingly different.
Finest quality boats.
Free colour brochure and route planner.
Ring 01327 340739

GUIDED WALKING TOURS
TREK AMERICA
Over 60 exciting treks from 7 days – 9 weeks, year round.
Phone 01295 256777
www.trekamerica.com
camping, walking and lodging tours

cycling and walking
Bicycle and walking tours
01568 780800

City tours
Over 1000 exciting cities.
Guided sightseeing tours.
Tel. 09356 55219

Worldwide adventures
Choose from over 200 trips to more than 90 countries.
• Wildlife Safaris • Jungle Exploration • Hikes
• Cultural Tours • Wilderness Experience
Call 01252 760 100 for a free colour brochure
www.explore.co.uk

The camping and caravanning club
For your free information pack call
024 7685 6797

Activity holidays
for 14 - 19 year olds
Choose from over 60 activities throughout the UK and France
For free colour brochure c...
0500 749 147
www.pgl.co.uk

Rock climbing courses
Beginners and experienced climbers.
24 hour answering service
01752 698315

Fun Park
For details ring
01233 647033

Arctic adventure
An unforgettable holiday including jeep excursions and snowmobile tours.
06447 35601

8

Skimming advertisements / making telephone enquiries **A3**

2. A survey

Interview your partner to find out what kind of holidays he or she likes, then report back to the rest of the class:

a) What kind of holiday do you prefer? 1. Active holidays with lots of sports .... ❑ 2. Lying on a beach, sunbathing and swimming .. ❑ 3. Sightseeing trips .... ❑ 4. Walking or cycling tours............... ❑ **b)** Do you like staying in one place or touring around? Why? **c)** Would you like to go camping? Why/Why not? **d)** If money were no problem where would you like to go on holiday? What would you do there?	**e)** Would you prefer to go alone or with someone else? **f)** If you only had room in your suitcase for one of these things which would you take? 1. The latest best-seller .... ❑ 2. Your camera .... ❑ 3. A guidebook......................... ❑ **g)** How would you spend a free afternoon in London? 1. Go on one of the walks in the guidebook..... ❑ 2. Sit somewhere and just watch people .... ❑ 3. Go for a boat ride on the Thames.......... ❑

Now report to the class:

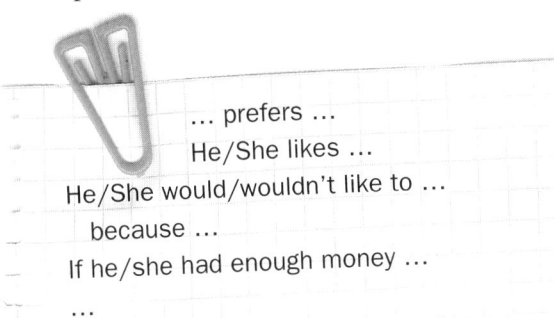

... prefers ...
He/She likes ...
He/She would/wouldn't like to ...
  because ...
If he/she had enough money ...
  ...

3. Making enquiries

Read the adverts in detail and choose one which interests you. With your partner make up a phone call in which you ask for more details. Take it in turns to be the person asking for information.

Person in office: Hello, how can I help you?
You: Hello, this is ... speaking. I wanted to ask about/ I'm interested in ...
Your partner: Right. What would you like to know?
You: ...

Where ...? When ...? How/What about ...? Is there ...? How much ...? Could I ...? Do ...? How ...? Would you please send me ...?	Would I have to ...? When is the next ...? Do I need a passport for ...? Is ... included? What kind of activities ...? How far do they go on the ... tours? Would I have to buy ...? How old are the people on the ... holiday, usually?	Well, thank you very much. That was very helpful. You're welcome. Would you like (me) to ...?

A4 Skimming with the help of illustrations and headings / making notes (table)

1. Skimming for the general idea

Before you read this extract from a travel guide to New York write down some things you already know about the city.

Then get a general idea of what the extract is about by looking through it, or 'skimming' through it, quickly.

Write down some questions you expect to be answered. Which parts of the text would you read to find this information?

TIPS
- Use heading, subheadings and illustrations to get a general idea of what a text is about.
- Think of what you expect from the text.
- Try to remember what you already know.

★★★ **NEW YORK** ★★★

THE BEGINNING

New York, also known as the 'Big Apple', is a city which is constantly changing. It is very difficult to imagine what it was like a century ago and almost impossible to picture it when it first came into existence as the trading station Nieuw Amsterdam, built by Dutch settlers in 1625. The name was changed to New York by the British, when they captured it in 1664.

New York City began as a sea port. In those days the whole of its coastline was full of ships of all kinds – cargo boats, trans-Atlantic liners, warships, ferries, pleasure boats, police launches and fishing boats. This constant sea traffic made the waterways look like today's congested motorways. Now, when we think of New York, we do not immediately associate it with shipping. Indeed, a stranger to the city might hardly realize that it is a port at all, since the sea is blocked out by solid walls of skyscrapers. But although shipping is no longer so important, New York still functions as a port and has the largest harbour in the US.

A CITY GROWS

New York City grew rapidly and by 1790 it was the largest city in the US with a population of about 33,000. In 1898 five districts joined together – Manhattan, Brooklyn, Queens, Bronx and Staten Island – which boosted the population to around 3.4 million. Another reason for this increase was the influx[1] of immigrants, mostly from Europe. Between 1815 and 1914 about 35 million people emigrated to the US. From 1892–1924 the main entry point was Ellis Island in New York Bay.

A MULTICULTURAL CITY

Today New York streets are a lively mix of about 7 million mainly English-speaking Americans, whose ancestors[2] came firstly from Europe and later Asia, South and Central America, Africa and the Pacific and Caribbean islands. During the last century the population has changed enormously from an almost all-white majority to a colourful mixture (see graph).

New York City 1900–2000. Percentage of population by race and Hispanic origin.

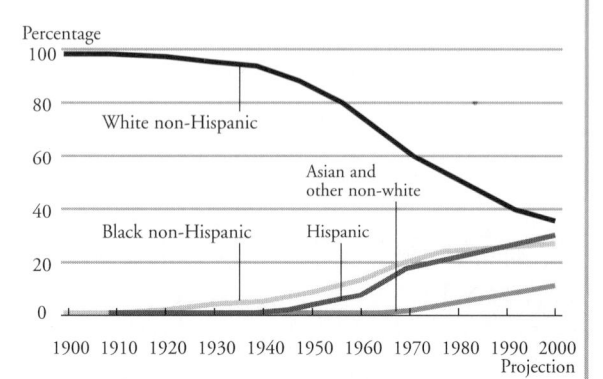

Source: U.S. Census; New York City Department of City Planning

Skimming with the help of illustrations and headings / making notes (table) — A 4

The influx of immigrants has been tremendously[3] valuable to the city since they brought with them new skills and different styles of music, dress and cooking.

THINGS TO DO

New York offers a huge choice of things to do and see. Most tourists like to visit the Statue of Liberty, the symbol of freedom and opportunity which has always welcomed everyone entering the port. Other favourites are the Empire State Building, the Rockefeller Center, Chinatown, Greenwich Village, Broadway, Times Square and Fifth Avenue.

New York has always been the entertainments capital of the world and there is an enormous range of theatres, museums, art galleries and cultural events for every taste.

GETTING AROUND

Visitors to New York usually stay in Manhattan, where most of the sights are. Finding your way around on foot is easy because the streets and avenues have numbers rather than names. The streets run from east to west and the avenues north to south. Alternatively, there is a good subway system, buses and taxis.

Vocabulary: 1 *influx* – sudden arrival of large numbers of people; 2 *ancestors* – *here:* those who arrived before (Vorfahren); 3 *tremendously* – enormously

2. Reading for detail

Read the article more carefully. Write down any answers you found to your questions. Were they all answered? Do you have any new ones now?

3. Making notes

Find the most important information in the first three paragraphs, underline it and put it into this table.
Use your own words as well as those from the text.

TIP
To make information easier to locate put it into table form.

History	Growth up to 1924	Population today

4. The contribution of immigrants

Immigrants have made a huge contribution to the rich culture of New York, and the USA altogether. Make a list of things in your own country which have been taken over from other cultures. Think, for example, of food and music.

A 5 Reading and writing book descriptions ('blurbs')

1. Choosing a book

When we choose books to read we usually look at their covers and read the description ('blurb') written on the back.

Look at these various blurbs. Do not read them in detail, just skim through them.

Then check how good a reader you are by answering the questions.

TIP
Practise picking up as much information as you can in a short time.

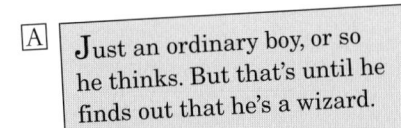

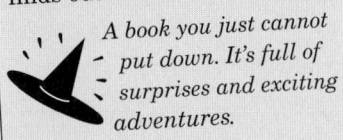

A Just an ordinary boy, or so he thinks. But that's until he finds out that he's a wizard.
A book you just cannot put down. It's full of surprises and exciting adventures.

B
• Why do you dream?
• Why do the stars shine?
The answers to these questions and hundreds more are in this book.
A wonderful new children's encyclopedia.

C A red card for any football fan who doesn't put this on their bookshelf.
Packed with lovely pictures, facts and opinions about your favourite football stars.
Get your Football Annual NOW!

D The funniest collection of jokes and cartoons you have ever seen.
Question:
What goes "ha, ha, ha, PLOP"?
Answer:
Someone laughing her head off.

E Strangers meet at a party. After only four minutes they know if they can be friends – or more?
A teacher comes into a classroom, says a few words and suddenly everyone sits up and listens.
Here's how to make these first four minutes work for YOU.

F The fascinating story of a one-legged fanatic, Captain Ahab, who swears to kill the white whale that has crippled him. 
One of the greatest adventure stories ever told.

G A good detective finds all sorts of clues to catch a criminal.
These stories in this book show you how detectives work –
• how to read clues,
• recognise handwriting and
• make identikit pictures.

H The need to understand the basic principles of science has never been greater.
This *new encyclopedia* explains scientific principles so that a child can understand them.

I Really funny stories about really stupid criminals.
Have you heard about:
- The bank robbers who left their map in the bank, showing where they were going?
- The thief who left his dog at a house he had broken into. When the police found the dog it took them straight home.

1. Which different kinds of books are described?
2. Are there any encyclopedias?
3. Is there a children's encyclopedia?
4. What is one of the novels about?
5. Are there any funny books?
6. One of the books is about people's behaviour in everyday life. What does it describe?
7. Are there any books about hobbies or sports?

Reading and writing book descriptions ('blurbs') A 5

2. Your choice

Find out what kind of books your partner likes.
Take it in turns to ask:

– Which book would you choose? Why?
– Which books would not interest you at all? Why not?

Then report back to the class.

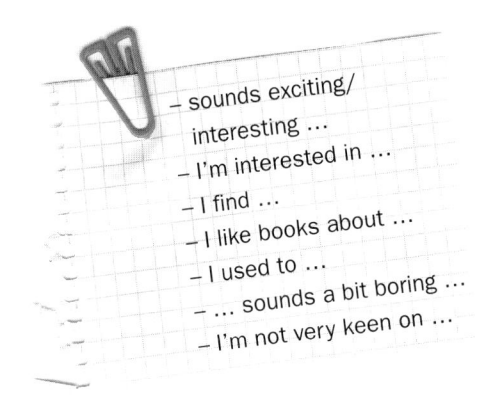

– sounds exciting/interesting …
– I'm interested in …
– I find …
– I like books about …
– I used to …
– … sounds a bit boring …
– I'm not very keen on …

3. Which would you prefer?

Which of these books would you prefer to read? Give your reasons.

She had been told again and again by her mother that she must never use her secret power to make objects move – not even little tricks like putting out a candle or locking a door.

But one day the girls at school laughed at her once too often and she fought back, releasing her tremendous power and transforming a small, quiet New England town into a holocaust of destruction.

*This story will terrify you,
but you will not be able to put it down.*

AN ADVENTURE STORY …

A group of schoolboys, all under 13 except one, is shipwrecked on a Pacific island after a plane crash. Alone on the island, they have to find a way of surviving.
Two of them, Ralph and Jack, take charge. Whereas Ralph tries to set up a democratic society, Jack is more interested in making rules and giving out punishment.

The story explodes the myth that young children are pure and innocent, as the boys' society gradually falls into violence and anarchy.

… with a deeper message

4. My suggestion

Think of a book or film which you really enjoyed.
Write a description of it, like the blurbs you have just read.
Make it sound so good that others will want to read or see it.
Be careful though, do not spoil the story by writing too much.

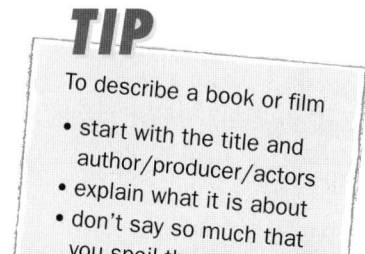

TIP
To describe a book or film
- start with the title and author/producer/actors
- explain what it is about
- don't say so much that you spoil the story

– … *(title)*, by … *(author)* is a great …
– It is about/It tells the story of …
– You learn a lot about …
– It is so interesting/It explains …
– It gives you lots of information about …
– It really makes you laugh
– really funny/the funniest

– One of the greatest …
– The … you have ever read/seen
– You can't put it down
– It's full of surprises and exciting adventures
– wonderful, fascinating
– lovely pictures

Put all the descriptions in a box and mix them up. Everyone takes one.

Does your description make you want to read the book or see the film. Why? Why not?

A6 Scanning an advertisement / explaining (sports) rules in writing

1. Finding specific information

Read this advertisement to find out which sports are offered on each day of the week. Write down all the possibilities in the diary.

TIP: Do not read details, only look for the information you need.

TRAFFORD SPORTS CENTRE

JUNIOR FOOTBALL
11–18 years: Sat: 1.00 pm – 2.00 pm.
£3.00

SWIMMING
Mon. closed
Tues. – Sat: 9.00 am – 8.00 pm.
Sun: 10.00 am – 4.30 pm.
Ladies only: Wed. 8.00 pm – 9.00 pm.
Tues. – Fri.: £1.50
Sat., Sun.: £2.00

VOLLEYBALL
No need to book. Just come along.
Adults:
Wed: 7.00 pm – 9.00 pm. £3.60
Juniors:
13 – 18 year olds. Wed: 4.00 pm – 5.30 pm. £2.50

SQUASH
An 8-week course for *beginners*.
Fri: 7.30 pm – 9.00 pm.
£24

KARATE
Beginners class:
Mon. 6.30 pm – 7.45 pm.
Intermediate – Advanced:
Mon. 7.45 pm – 9.00 pm, Wed. 7.45 pm – 9.00 pm.
£3.00

BASKETBALL
Adults: Thurs: 7.30 pm – 9.00 pm.
Juniors: Sat: 9.00 am – 11.00 am.
No booking. £4.00

BADMINTON
Improve your game with 8 weeks of coaching.
Tues: 9.30 pm – 11.00 pm.
£24

JUDO
Tues: 8.30 pm – 9.30 pm.
Fri: 7.00 pm – 8.30 pm.
£3.60

AEROBICS
Mon: 6.00 pm – 7.00 pm.
Tues: 6.00 pm – 7.00 pm.
£2.80

GYMNASTICS
Mon: 8.45 am – 9.45 am.
9.45 am – 10.45 am.
£2.50

ROLLER DISCO
Skate to the latest sounds.
Sat: 2.00 pm – 4.00 pm.
£2.00

FITNESS CLUB
Lots of healthy fun, including jogging, rowing and cycling.
Sun: 2.00 pm – 4.00 pm.
£3.00

CHINESE KICKBOXING
Thurs: 5.00 pm – 6.30 pm.
£3.00

OPENING TIMES: Monday to Friday: 9.00 am – 10.00 pm • Saturday & Sunday: 9.00 am – 11.00 pm

---

Monday	Tuesday	Wednesday	Thursday	Friday	Saturday	Sunday

Scanning an advertisement / explaining (sports) rules in writing **A 6**

2. Asking for and giving information

Find a partner: one of you works at the sports centre, the other rings up and asks for some information. After two or three questions change roles.

3. Understanding rules

Match two rules to each sport or game and write the numbers under the correct heading.

1. There are two teams, each made up of five players.
2. There are six games in a set.
3. The ball can be replaced if it is lost.
4. The aim of the game is to win your opponent's king.
5. To start, the ball is thrown in the air and hit with the racket.
6. Players must make their moves in a given time.
7. Only one step can be taken while holding the ball.
8. A player can use up to fourteen clubs.

Write down five rules of your own for these sports and games or different ones. Can your partner guess which ones you mean?

4. Explaining rules

These rules for a popular game are no good to anyone because they are in the wrong order. Can you sort them out? Decide first on the best order.

What is the game?

Players can only hold the ball for a maximum of three seconds and cannot take more than three steps while holding it. There are two teams of 5 or 7 players, a time-keeper and two referees. The aim is to score as many goals as possible.

This team game is similar to football and basketball. The only person allowed in the goal area is the goalkeeper. A game lasts for an hour and has two 30-minute halves. It begins when one player throws the ball to a member of his or her team from the centre of the court. It is usually played indoors, on a court with a goal at each end. Except for the goalkeeper players are not allowed to kick the ball.

The ball is round and slightly smaller than a football. They throw and bounce it towards the goal, stopping and hitting it with any part of the body except the lower legs and feet. It can be passed in any direction and also rolled along the ground.

Think of one of your favourite sports or games and write down the rules for playing it, but keep its name secret. Then check how good your instructions are by reading them out to the class. Do they know what you are describing?

A7 Scanning an encyclopedia article / making notes (list)

1. Before you start reading

Check how much you know about Canada. Mark the questions you cannot answer.

Then write down anything else you know about Canada. What would you like to know?

TIP
Before you read new information try to remember what you already know about the subject.

1. How many of Canada's provinces or territories can you name?

   _____

2. Is Canada
   larger than the US. .... ❏
   or smaller than the US? .... ❏

3. Where do most Canadians live:
   spaced out evenly over the whole country .... ❏
   or concentrated in certain areas? .... ❏

4. How many time zones are there in Canada?

5. What do you know about the country's political system?

   _____

6. Which is the other main language spoken in Quebec besides English?

   _____

2. Looking for specific information

Quickly read through this article to find the answers you did not know.

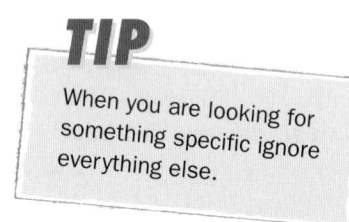

TIP
When you are looking for something specific ignore everything else.

CANADA

Canada is the world's second largest country after Russia. It stretches over five time zones and is divided into ten provinces (Alberta, British Columbia, Manitoba, New Brunswick, Newfoundland, Nova Scotia, Ontario, Prince Edward Island, Quebec, Saskatchewan) and three territories (the Northwest Territory, Yukon Territory and Nunavut).

About three quarters of Canada's 30 million people inhabit a relatively narrow strip of land along the US border, concentrated in Quebec and Ontario. The three territories, vast areas of land, are very empty with only 0.3 per cent of the total population. The population as a whole is mostly urban, living in the main cities of Toronto, Montreal, Winnipeg, Calgary, Edmonton, Vancouver and Ottawa, the capital.

For centuries Canada was inhabited by Inuits (Eskimos) and Indians. But from the sixteenth century onwards the British and French began to settle and to fight for power. Today nearly 40 per cent of Canadians have British origins, 27 per cent French, 16 per cent Asian and the remainder are a rich ethnic mix of Germans, Italians, Ukrainians, Dutch, Scandinavians, Poles, Hungarians, Greeks and the native peoples, officially known as the 'First nations' (3 per cent). During the past thirty years Canada's ethnic mix has changed significantly, mainly because of a more open policy towards immigrants. The government encourages each ethnic group to preserve their own culture.

Canada has two official languages, English and French. Most French-speaking Canadians live in Quebec, where they make up about 78 per cent of the 7 million inhabitants. They feel quite distinct from the rest of the country and are proud of their language and culture, constantly trying to defend it from further anglicization. This has been reflected in a desire for independence from Canada and in growing support for pro-separatist parties.

Canada is a country with enormous natural resources, notably oil, gas, minerals, forests, huge lakes and rivers. It is the world's largest exporter

Scanning an encyclopedia article / making notes (list) **A7**

of forest products and a main exporter of fish, furs, wheat and hydro-electricity. It is also an important manufacturing country. Whereas up to the twentieth century the economy was largely based on agriculture, today Canada is one of the most highly industrialized countries in the world.

Politically speaking, Canada is a federal constitutional monarchy and a member of the Commonwealth. The head of state is Britain's Queen Elizabeth II (from 1952 onwards), represented by a Governor-General with formal duties only. The head of government is the prime minister.

Did the article tell you what you wanted to know or are there still some things you will have to find out for yourself?

3. Identifying the main points

Read the whole article carefully to get the general idea. Then read it again and underline or highlight the main points.

Compare your results.

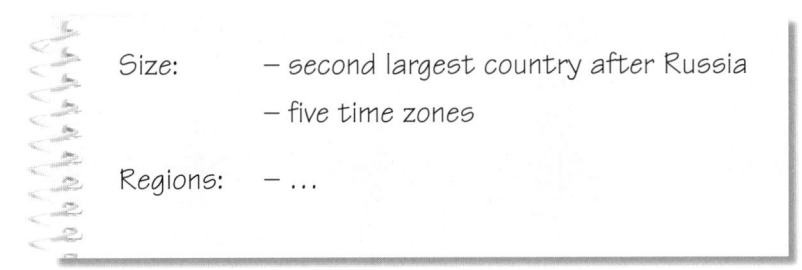

TIP
It is easier to locate information in a text if you mark the main points.

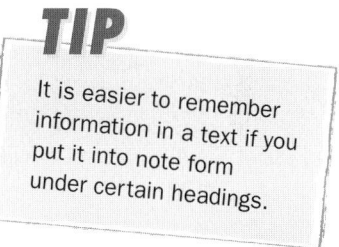

4. Putting information into note form

Reduce the main points to notes, using words from the text or your own. Then group them together under certain headings. You may want to change the order of the information to fit in with your categories.

TIP
It is easier to remember information in a text if you put it into note form under certain headings.

```
Size:      – second largest country after Russia
           – five time zones

Regions:   – ...
```

5. Checking what you have learned

Working in pairs, make up a quiz on Canada. Write down about 8 questions. Then exchange papers.

Give the papers back and mark the answers. Who got everything right?

A8 Writing informal letters

1. Introducing yourself to a stranger

Imagine you see this letter on the school notice-board.

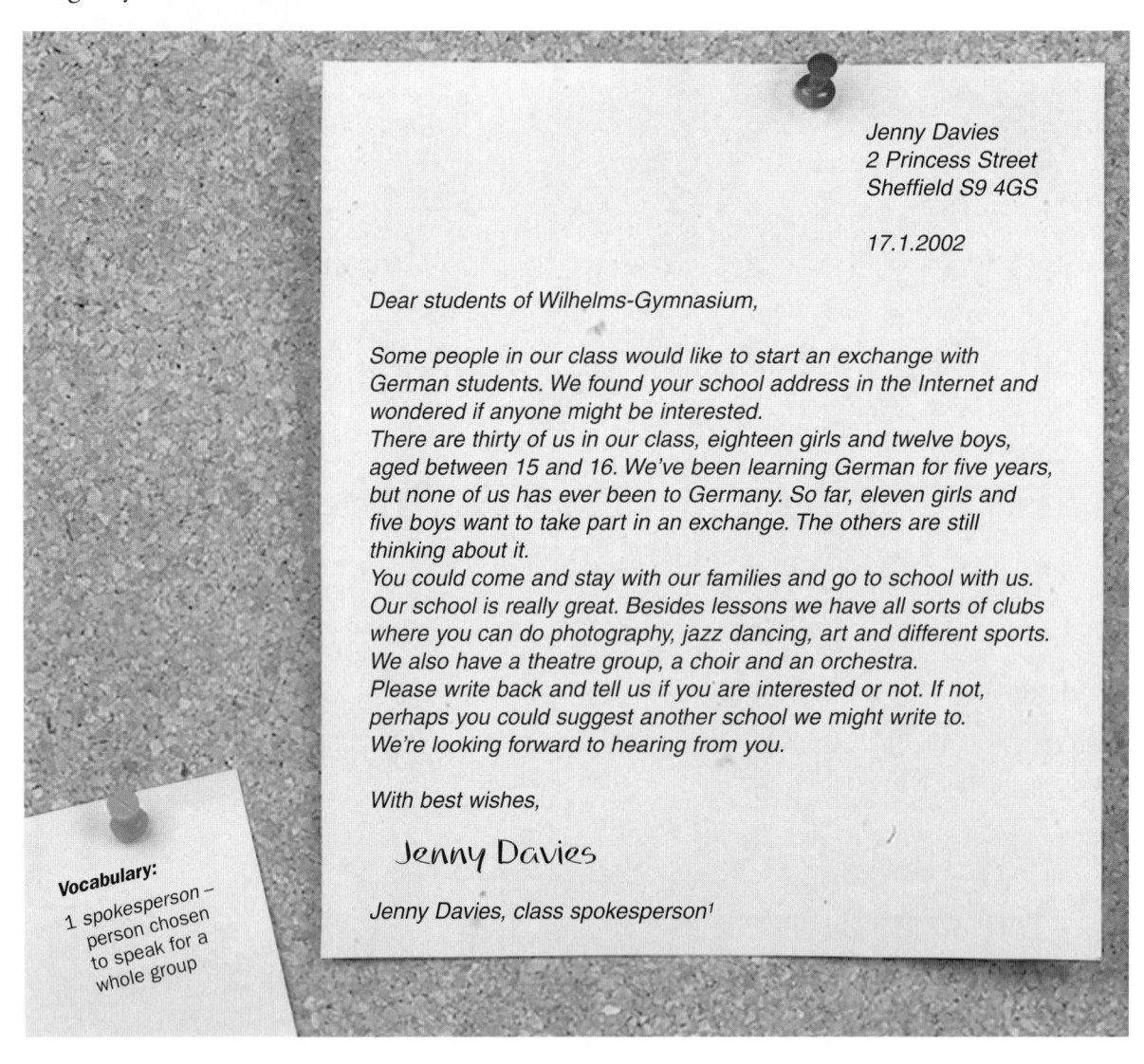

> Jenny Davies
> 2 Princess Street
> Sheffield S9 4GS
>
> 17.1.2002
>
> Dear students of Wilhelms-Gymnasium,
>
> Some people in our class would like to start an exchange with German students. We found your school address in the Internet and wondered if anyone might be interested.
> There are thirty of us in our class, eighteen girls and twelve boys, aged between 15 and 16. We've been learning German for five years, but none of us has ever been to Germany. So far, eleven girls and five boys want to take part in an exchange. The others are still thinking about it.
> You could come and stay with our families and go to school with us. Our school is really great. Besides lessons we have all sorts of clubs where you can do photography, jazz dancing, art and different sports. We also have a theatre group, a choir and an orchestra.
> Please write back and tell us if you are interested or not. If not, perhaps you could suggest another school we might write to.
> We're looking forward to hearing from you.
>
> With best wishes,
>
> *Jenny Davies*
>
> Jenny Davies, class spokesperson[1]

Vocabulary:
1 spokesperson – person chosen to speak for a whole group

Write back to Jenny, telling her you would like to take part in the exchange.

Before you start writing note down what you want to say, e.g.:

- my interests: _____
- our school: _____
- my family: _____
- best time to visit: _____

Pick out some phrases from Jenny's letter which are useful for making suggestions and asking for something.

Writing informal letters **A 8**

2. Writing an informal letter

Informal letters are the kind you write to friends, your family or people you know quite well. Young people also write informally to strangers if they are the same age.

Your letter should look like this.

> Your address goes in the top right-hand corner. (Leave it out for people you know well.)

> Leave 1 line before the date, under your address.

> Start with *Dear* .... Put a comma after it.

> Begin the first sentence with a capital letter.

> Short forms of verbs can be used in informal letters (but not in formal ones).

> End with *Best wishes,* / *All the best,* / *See you soon,* / *Love,* (only for people you know very well). Put a comma after the ending.

Dates

We can write the date in different ways, e.g.: Day – month – year: *17ᵗʰ January, 2002* (or *'02*)
Month – day – year: *January 17ᵗʰ, 2002*

– The letters after the numbers (*-th* / *-st* / *-nd* / *-rd*) can be left out, also the comma before the year.
– The longer months are often shortened, e.g. *Jan.* for 'January'.

The date can also be written completely in figures, e.g.: *8.9.2002* or *8.09.02*

– In British English (BE) this means 'September 8, 2002'.
– But in American English (AE) it means '9 August, 2002', because the number of the month is written before the day.

When we say the date we add *the* ('September *the* eighth') and *of* ('*the* eighth *of* September') in BE, but not in AE ('September eighth' or 'September eight').

A9 Writing formal letters: applying for jobs

1. Jobs

Have you ever had a job? If so, explain what you had to do and why you wanted the job. Was it because you needed the money or did you want to learn some specific skills?

Have you thought about the kind of job you would like to do after school? Take it in turns to find out how your partner feels.

Do you know what you're going to do after school?

> Have you thought about ...?
> Have you any idea what ...?

> ... thinks she might .../would like to .../ isn't sure yet/is planning to/ hasn't really thought about it yet/...

2. Can I help you?

Can you tell what jobs these people do from the things they say?

a) Anything to drink?
b) Open wide, please.
c) I've got a parcel for Mrs Watson.
d) I'd better put my make-up on. The show starts in ten minutes.
e) Smile please.
f) Is this your bike, miss?
g) Stay in bed for the next two days.
h) Keep your head up and kick your legs.
k) Anything else? Five pounds, then, please.

Can you think of some more yourself?

3. Applying for a job

You are looking for a holiday job for the summer and see this advertisement.

INTERNATIONAL SUMMER CAMP

Looking for a summer job?
Why not combine work with a holiday?
We need young people to work as

Holiday Hosts

at our international camp this summer.
If you speak good English, are cheerful and like working with children contact us. It would be an advantage if you can play a musical instrument or do sports.

Please enclose a photograph. Write to the Manager, South Sands Holiday Camp, Littlehampton BN17 5LF

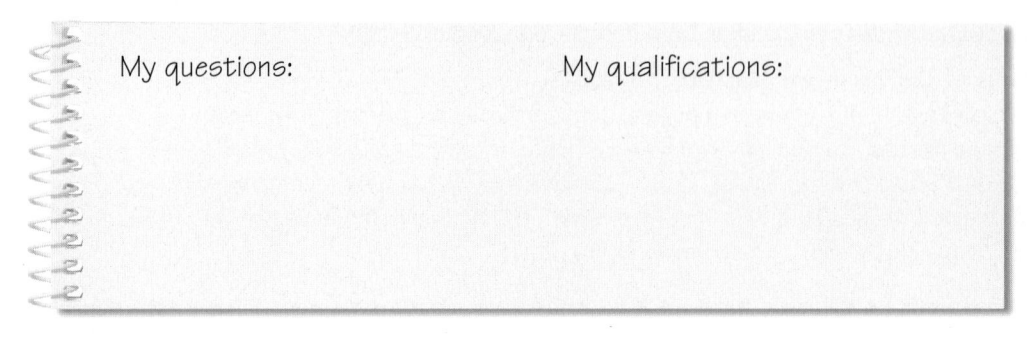

You are going to write and apply for the job. First make some notes:

– What do you want to know about the job?
– Why do you think you would be good at it?

My questions: My qualifications:

Writing formal letters: applying for jobs A 9

4. Writing formal letters

The appearance of a letter is very important, especially when you are applying for a job.

Use this model to write a letter, applying for a job as a holiday host.

TIP

Formal letters:
- Before 'Dear ...,' briefly give reason for writing.
- 'Dear Sir/Madam,' if you do not know who will open the letter.
- 'Dear Ms (Brown),' if you do not know if the woman is married.
- End with 'Yours sincerely,' if you do not know the person.

Sender's address in top right-hand corner; no commas at end of lines

Name and address of person you are writing to

Your address
....
....
....

The Manager
....
....
....

7/2/2001

Leave 1 line before date.

Leave 2–3 lines, then briefly explain your reason for writing.

Leave 1 line before the greeting, with a comma after it.

Application for a job as a holiday host

Dear Sir/Madam,

Leave 1 line.

Start with capital letter. Explain why you are writing.

I saw your advertisement for .../I am writing to
....
....
....
....

Leave 1 line between each paragraph. Do not make the paragraphs too long.

Leave 1–2 lines before ending, with comma after it.

Yours sincerely,

(name)

Leave 1 line before signing.

---

to apply for a job
to look after/entertain
good at/would like to
unfortunately
to play an instrument
Would you please give me/
I would be grateful for some information about ...
to have experience as/of working with

cheerful sort of person
to get on well with/to enjoy
have been learning English for
would be able to teach the children how to
Do you provide ...?/Could you help me with/
Could you help me to find ...?
working hours/pay/accomodation

A 10 An informative text / reorganising information

1. Picking out information

Read this article about Australia and pick out the information you need to label the map.

Australia

Together with the nearby island of Tasmania, Australia forms the smallest continent, although it is one of the largest countries in the world, covering about 7.6 million sq km, including Tasmania. From the Indian Ocean to the west and the Pacific Ocean to the east Australia has a huge variety of landscapes, including tropical rainforests, deserts, snow-capped mountains and wide areas of farmland. Some areas are so dry that they can only be used for grazing sheep, such as the interior ('outback') of the north eastern state of Queensland, its southern neighbour New South Wales and South Australia.

Most of the population of 18 million (the official 1996 estimate) live in one of the main cities of Brisbane, Canberra, Sydney, Melbourne, Perth, Darwin or Adelaide. These cities are spread over huge areas and two out of three Australians live in one of their suburbs. All of them except Canberra, Australia's capital, are on the coast. The largest and most famous city is Sydney, the capital of New South Wales. Sydney became world famous when it held the 2000 Olympic Games. It has the largest surburban area in the world, twice as big as Bejing and six times the size of Rome. In 1995 the official population estimate was nearly 4 million. Outside the cities, the remaining 97 per cent of Australia is almost completely uninhabited. Most of the 15 per cent of the rural population has settled along the narrow fertile[1] strip running from Queensland's capital Brisbane, along the coasts of New South Wales and Victoria and on round to Adelaide, the capital of the state of South Australia.

Australia has much to offer visitors, from the rich cultural life of cities like Sydney and Melbourne, the capital of Victoria, to skiing in the Australian Alps, which rise to their highest point at Mount Kosciusko (2,228 m) in New South Wales. One hugely popular attraction is the Great Barrier Reef, which runs parallel to Queensland's coast for almost 2,000 kilometres. Made of coral and with its clear waters, algae, sponges and countless species of fish, it is a wonderful place for snorkelling and diving. In recent years the town of Cairns, the gateway to the Reef, has expanded tremendously[2] due to[3] an increase in tourism. Tourists also enjoy the sights of the Northern Territory – the capital Darwin and, in the outback, the town of Alice Springs and Uluru (Ayers Rock), the world's largest monolith at the centre of the whole continent.

Sydney Opera House

Great Barrier Reef

Besides tourism, Australia's economy also relies on income from its mineral wealth. The state of Western Australia, which is larger than the whole of Western Europe (2,527,621 sq km), produces 11 per cent of the world's iron ore and over 60 per cent of Australia's gold. It has one of the largest known deposits of natural gas and is one of the most important sources of diamonds in the world. Perth, the state capital, is Australia's fourth largest city, but also its most isolated.

Uluru (Ayers Rock)

Vocabulary: 1 *fertile* – good enough (land) to grow things; 2 *tremendously* – enormously; 3 *due to* – because of

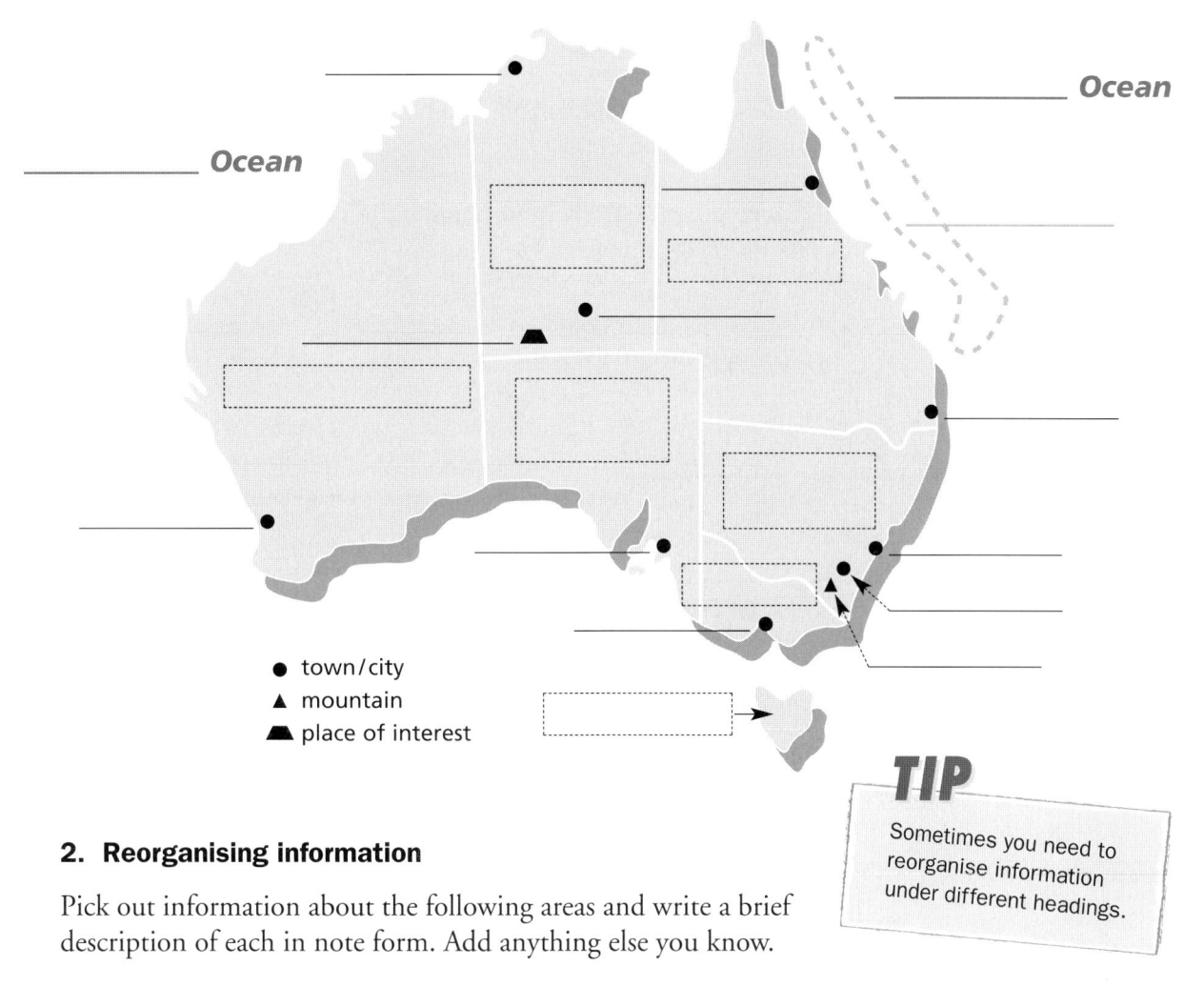

An informative text / reorganising information **A 10**

_____ Ocean

_____ Ocean

- ● town/city
- ▲ mountain
- ▲ place of interest

2. Reorganising information

Pick out information about the following areas and write a brief description of each in note form. Add anything else you know.

TIP
Sometimes you need to reorganise information under different headings.

Queensland	South Australia
interior dry, used for grazing sheep	
	Victoria
New South Wales	Northern Territory
	Western Australia

3. Check what you have learned

Cover the article up and write down five questions about Australia. Find a partner and take it in turns to ask one question. Do not look at the text until all ten questions have been asked.

Did you get everything right? If not check the answers with the text.

A 11 — Conventional features of instructional texts / writing instructions

1. Could you give first aid?

Would you know what to do in an accident? Could you give first aid in these situations? What shouldn't you do?

1. Someone in your family spills boiling water on their arm.

2. You are playing volleyball and someone gets a cramp in the leg.

2. Changing prose into a set of instructions

What do you think about the way these instructions are written?

> In an accident it is important to act quickly. The most important thing is not to waste any time, but to give first aid immediately to stop the injury from getting worse. When you have done this you must get help as quickly as possible. While you are waiting for help to arrive you should try to make the patient as comfortable as you can. But you have to be careful. If you think something might be broken you should not move them at all.

Rewrite them so that they are easier to read in an emergency.
An idea for a beginning:

> In an accident it is important to act quickly:
> 1. Give first aid <u>immediately</u> to ...

3. Characteristic features of instructions

Compare your set of instructions with the one in task 2. List the ways in which you have made them clearer and easier to read.

Type of sentences: _____

Verb forms: _____

Layout: _____

Look at these instructions for giving first aid to someone who has fainted. Would they help you to act in an emergency? Is there anything else you would need to know?

> **Fainting**
> If someone looks as if they are going to faint open a window or take them into the fresh air. If they faint the best thing is to try to lay them down somewhere. Raise the legs so that they are higher than the head.

Conventional features of instructional texts / writing instructions A11

4. Writing a set of instructions

These first aid instructions are far too complicated to read in an emergency. Rewrite them as a poster.

Decide whether there should be any illustrations.
If you need more than one number them to show which part of the text they illustrate.

How to treat simple injuries

The first thing to do if someone has had an accident is to find out exactly what is wrong. It is important not to panic because by staying calm you help the injured person to relax. Then you should ask if the person feels there is anything wrong, for instance that they cannot move an arm or a leg. You have to look for clues, for instance whether the skin is cold and sweaty or hot and dry or whether the face is very pale or red. There might be blood somewhere, too.

If someone faints it is good if you can recognise the signs before it actually happens. Usually the face goes pale and the skin is sweaty. The person feels weak and sometimes sick, too. You should lay them down and raise their legs a little so the blood flows towards the brain. You should make sure there is plenty of fresh air. When they start to feel better help them to sit up, but very slowly.

If your nose bleeds sit down and bend slightly over a sink or bowl to catch the blood. You should breathe through your mouth and hold your nose between your fingers and thumb at the top end of the nose. Sometimes you have to press for up to ten minutes. It helps to undo any tight clothing round the neck. Then soak a piece of cloth (or a hanky) in cold water and put it over the top of the nose. It is important not to tilt your head back because the blood will run down your throat and make you choke. You should not push anything up your nose, like cotton wool. When the bleeding has stopped you should try not to blow your nose for a few hours because that might start the bleeding again.

If you have a bruise put some ice in a plastic bag and leave it on the bruise for about half an hour. (If there is no ice you can use a bag of frozen peas).

Use headings like this for your poster:

+ FIRST AID +
Treating simple injuries
...

TIPS
- Use short, easy sentences.
- Address the reader directly by using imperatives.
- Divide the information into small, clear steps and number them.
- Put the steps in the correct order.
- Do not miss anything out. Include any warnings.
- Emphasize important words by capital letters or heavy type.
- Illustrations help to make explanations clearer. They may need numbering.

When you have finished exchange your work with other students. Perhaps you can make suggestions for improvements?

A 12 Identifying the main ideas in a newspaper article / linking ideas

1. Talking about spending money

Do you ever think about how you spend your pocket money?
Do you save any?

What do you spend your pocket money on?
Fill in this table.

Food/soft drinks	%	Transport	%
Leisure goods	%	Leisure services	%
Clothing	%	Personal goods	%

- *Leisure goods*: things needed for hobbies, sports, entertainments etc.
- *Leisure services*: tickets for concerts, discos; membership of sports clubs etc.
- *Personal goods*: shampoo, cosmetics, perfume etc.

Is there a significant difference between the spending habits of the boys and the girls in your class?

2. A comparison with British teenagers

Skim through the article to get a general idea of the contents. Then read it more carefully and underline the main ideas. Reduce what you have underlined to a few key words and circle them.

Give each paragraph a heading.

TIPS

Identify main ideas by:
- Underlining important parts, then reducing them to key words or phrases.
- Thinking of headings for each paragraph.

Kids with money in their pockets

Carol Maitland
Social Affairs Correspondent

According to a recent survey, British teenagers have on average £8.30 a week spending money. Most of it, up to £3.20 a week, goes on food – sweets, crisps, soft drinks, ice cream and school meals. Next come leisure goods such as CDs and sports gear[1], averaging about £2.00 a week. The third most popular item is clothing.

Whilst boys and girls spend roughly the same amount of money, they tend to use it differently. Boys need most of it for food, leisure goods and leisure services. Although girls spend almost the same amount on food, they use nearly twice as much as boys for clothes. They also spend twice as much on personal goods such as toiletries[2], make-up and jewelry, averaging around 80p per week compared with only 40p for boys.

Most of the young people interviewed recognised the importance of managing their money properly. Indeed, they seem very skilled in making their incomes last as long as possible, hunting for bargains in second-hand shops and looking out for special offers. Another finding was that they were all very much aware of the influence of advertising. Steve, for instance, said, "I don't buy things just because they are fashionable. My money goes on day-to-day living, nothing extravagant."

How they spend it

	Boys	Girls
Food/soft drinks	£3.20	£3.10
Leisure goods	£2.10	£1.50
Clothing	£0.80	£1.50
Transport	£0.80	£1.00
Leisure services	£0.90	£0.60
Personal goods	£0.40	£0.80

Where parents were the main source of income there was sometimes resentment[3] if they wanted to know how the money was spent. Yet some youngsters welcomed their parents' involvement. "If I go shopping I know my mum will want to know what I've bought," said Soraya, "and that's good because it stops me from buying things I'll regret later."

Whereas some teenagers manage on the pocket money they get from their parents, others prefer to earn their own. Hossain, for example, explained, "If you go into the real world and get yourself a job, that's when you're independent. If you don't work for your money it's not really yours." Again and again it became clear that

Identifying the main ideas in a newspaper article / linking ideas **A12**

money means much more to young people than simply buying things. One girl pointed out, "Money makes you feel independent even if you are not. When you're out shopping by yourself and you've got some money in your pocket you feel independent."

Many teenagers find it unfair to expect their parents to pay for everything and so they get part-time jobs. Others want to help their family. One such person is Katie, "I pay my share of the phone bill at home. I think when you get older you should pay for it yourself." There was, however, a general consensus about parental responsibility. "If parents see a child isn't reliable," said Sandra, "he or she shouldn't have money of their own. They might go out and buy things like drugs."

Adapted from:
The Independent, 23.7.1997

Vocabulary: 1 *gear* – equipment, the things you need to do something; 2 *toiletries* – things connected with personal hygiene; 3 *resentment* – anger about something you find unfair

3. Recognising more and less important ideas

Look at this sentence from the article:

> Steve, for instance, said, "I don't buy things just because they are fashionable."

Which words show you that the sentence is not a main idea, but a less important one?

Words and phrases which connect ideas are called 'link-words', like *for example, and, but*. Find the link-word *indeed* in the article and explain its function.

TIP
Link-words show how ideas relate to each other.

Look for more link-words in the article and match them with their functions:

A. To contrast ideas or to contradict what has been said before: _but,_ _____

B. To list a number of ideas: _____

C. To explain a consequence: _____

D. To introduce examples or illustrations: _____

E. To underline or rephrase what has already been said: _____

Can you add any more link-words to each group?

4. Your opinion

How do you feel about pocket money?

Do you think young people should pay for certain things themselves?

Suggest ways of earning extra money.

TIPS
1. Note down all your ideas.
2. Group them together and order them logically.
3. Write a few paragraphs expressing your opinion. Put each main idea into a new paragraph. Give examples to support them.
4. Use link words to connect the ideas logically. Vary them to make your style more interesting.

A 13   Argumentative text / writing a balanced argument

1. Thinking about different points of view

How would you like to go to school dressed like this?

Think of some reasons why it might be a good idea and some arguments against it.

Arguments for school uniform	Arguments against school uniform
...	...

How many of you are in favour of school uniform? How many are against it?

Read this article from a school magazine and see if there are any more arguments which you can add to your table.

— City School Magazine —

School uniform?

By Tina and Tim, your up-to-the-minute reporters

Lately there has been a lot of debate about whether we should go back to wearing school uniform again, like they used to here.

Those who support the idea believe there would be fewer problems if we all wore the same clothes. Some schools which have introduced uniforms say fewer clothes are stolen and that their students' work has improved. This might be because they can concentrate better if they don't have to worry about their clothes all the time.

School uniform not only takes pressure off the students. Many parents cannot afford the fashionable clothes their children demand in order to 'belong'. A uniform would help these families to save money because their children's own clothes would not wear out so fast. Poorer families could be given financial help to buy the uniform. If everyone wore the same no one would know if the children came from a wealthy or a poorer background. So neither the students nor the parents would be embarrassed. Another advantage of school uniform is that the students would probably behave better in the street if everyone could see which school they went to. It would not be as easy to just stay away from school either. A further argument in favour of school uniform is that it creates a sense of belonging, making everyone feel they are part of one big family.

However, not everyone is in favour of school uniform. Many young people feel it would be boring to have to wear the same kind of clothes every day. Others point out that if they did not choose their own clothes they could not express their personality. They also say that the colour or style may not suit everyone. Another argument which is sometimes heard is that young people cannot be protected against social inequality and that they just have to learn to live with it.

Although we understand why some people are against school uniform, we have come to the conclusion that there are more arguments in favour of it. After all, without a uniform there is just as much pressure to conform because everyone feels forced to wear the latest brand-name clothes.

Have any of you changed your minds? If so, why?
Suggest some ways to stop jealousy over fashionable clothes.

Argumentative text / writing a balanced argument **A13**

2. Presenting both sides of the argument

Examine how the argument is presented by filling in this frame. Give each of the four sections of the text a heading.

You are going to write your own article discussing school uniform. Collect words and phrases from the text which would be useful for each section (some can be used in two), then add more of your own.

1. _____

2. _____

3. _____

4. _____

3. Writing a balanced argument

Without reading the article again write a short article discussing the question 'Should we wear school uniform or not?'.

If you want to persuade people to agree with your ideas you should be fair: explain both sides of the argument in a balanced way.

TIPS

1. Introduce the topic.
2. Give arguments for the proposal (with examples).
3. Give arguments against it (examples).
4. Explain your conclusion.
5. Check:
   - Are the ideas linked clearly?
   - Have you given a balanced view?
   - Is the vocabulary varied?

A14 Oral presentation of written texts / making notes, summarising

1. For and against 'Denglish'

Read this article on 'Denglish' and underline or circle the main points. Guess the meaning of any new words.

Can I use your handy, please?

Oh, you mean my 'mobile phone'?! Yes, of course. I've always got it handy.

DENGLISH

Since the beginning of the 1990s more and more English words and expressions have come into the German language, making it quite difficult to understand at times. Older people often cannot interpret what their children or grandchildren say. This is not a new development, every generation creates its own jargon, but there has been nothing quite like this latest phenomenon. English, or rather a jumbled[1] mixture of English and German known as 'Denglish', is rapidly dominating every walk of life – fashion, music, the media, sports, business, technology, advertising. One striking example is Lufthansa's advertisement 'Mit dem neuen Standby oneway Upgrade-Voucher kann direkt beim Check-in das Ticket aufgewertet werden' which hardly includes any German at all.

Although some people are horrified at the increasing influence of English on German, others argue that since language is a living thing change is a natural state. All languages borrow from each other and German is no exception. Whereas it previously borrowed from Latin, Greek and French, now it is from English. Often this is unavoidable, for example when new developments are taken over from a different culture and there are no words to describe them in the native language. At other times it is more practical to use the foreign word. Imagine, for instance, having to describe *spaghetti*. It is far easier to simply use the original than to order 'those long, thin noodles'. Some imported words have become so integrated that they are no longer regarded as foreign.

Many English words are preferred because of their brevity and succinctness[2], such as *stress* (shorter than 'Anstrengung'), *fast-food* or *workaholic*. However, today it appears that English expressions are not being borrowed for such practical reasons, but to demonstrate modernity or *coolness*. Why else should a local phone call be a *CityCall* and what is the advantage of calling a baker's a *Backshop*? The danger is not so much the flood of English words in itself, but rather the frequent mistakes, such as *last not least* instead of 'last but not least' or the introduction of the apostrophe *'s* into German, resulting in wrong usage such as '*Rudis'* Fundstube' or '*Info's* hier'. Some English words have been given different meanings to their original ones, for instance the *Handy*. In English this is not a noun, but an adjective, meaning 'useful'. The translation of the German 'Handy' is 'mobile phone'. Other examples are *Evergreen*, *Flipper* and *Oldtimer*. Some so-called 'English' words have simply been invented, although they do not actually exist in English. An English speaker, for instance, would not understand the word 'Backshop' and might think it was a shop around the back of a building, like 'back door', or even a shop where you can take things back if you do not like them. Other examples are *Dressman*, *Talkmaster* or *Wellness*. In other cases English and German have been combined to create new words, such as *anturnen, chatten, checken, relaxen*.

It can be argued that German is enriched by words from other languages and that 'Denglish' expresses the flexibility and openness of the German language and people. On the other hand, when words are wrongly used they do not contribute to international communication, as illustrated by the term 'Handy', which native speakers of English would not understand. Eventually Denglish results in a kind of pidgin English. And as to openness, other countries, including Britain and America, do not regard Germany as more modern or open because of their jumbled mixture of German and English. On the contrary, they find it rather ridiculous.

Many Germans oppose what they see as the public undermining of the German language, complaining that words like *clever, Event, happy, last minute, Highlight, Make-up, Power, relax, Sale, Shopping* and *Slow motion* have completely replaced their German equivalents. It has even been suggested that fines[3] be imposed, for instance, on taxi drivers displaying the English notice "Fasten your seat belt" instead of "Bitte anschnallen".

Vocabulary: 1 *jumbled* – confused; 2 *succinctness* – shortness and clarity; 3 *fine* – money paid as punishment for breaking a rule or law

Oral presentation of written texts / making notes, summarising — A14

2. Preparing a talk

You are going to give a short 3–4 minute talk on 'Denglish'.

– First pick out the parts of the article you want to use. Number them to put them in order, then list the main points in note form.

– Make notes for an introduction which will interest your listeners and also explain what your talk will be about. Perhaps start with an amazing fact, a rhetorical question or a problem. Memorize the beginning so you will be able to look at your audience.

– In note form sum up the main points and give your conclusion.

TIPS

Preparing a talk:
1. Make notes. Support arguments with examples.
2. Think of a good introduction and ending.

3. Giving the talk

Imagine your friend has to give a talk.
Think of a few tips to stop him or her from being nervous.

Good speakers help listeners to follow a talk and also make them feel involved. List some ways of doing this.

Before you start ...
Look ...
Try to ...

Helping listeners to follow the talk	Making the audience feel involved
– Speak _____	– Keep _____
– Check _____	– Check _____
– Use _____	– Encourage _____
– Do not _____	
– Vary _____	
– Write _____	

4. The audience's role

Before you speak in front of the class take it in turns to give your talk to a small group or a partner. During the talk listeners answer these questions and then make suggestions for improvements.

	YES	NO
– Is it a good introduction?	❏	❏
– Is the talk easy to follow? Are the steps logical?	❏	❏
– Do you feel involved? Does the speaker look at you or address you?	❏	❏
– Is there a good conclusion?	❏	❏

A 15 Debating / writing a poem

1. A survey

How do you feel about homework? Ask your partner:

1. Generally speaking, do you have a) too much homework?. . . . . ❏ b) not enough? . . . . ❏ c) about the right amount?. . . . . ❏	2. How much time do you spend on homework every day, roughly? a) Less than two hours . . . . ❏ b) More than two hours . . . . ❏ c) It is so different every day, I cannot say . . ❏

Now your partner interviews you. Report your results to the class:

> … says (s)he has/ doesn't have/ it's …

> (S)He spends roughly/ about … hours a day …/ can't say how much time…

2. Preparing for a debate

You are going to have a debate on 'The case for and against homework'. First think about the kind of homework you do. Is it usually preparing for the next lesson or summarising the last one? Which type of homework helps you most? What kind do you really hate?

Split the class into two halves: one half collects arguments in favour of homework, the other against it.

Arguments supporting homework	Arguments against homework

Take a vote on 'Should we have homework – yes or no?' and write down the result.

Debating / writing a poem A15

3. Debating behaviour

A discussion has to be orderly, so set out some rules for your debate.

Listen — *Don't* — *Let* — *If* — *You shouldn't*

4. The debate

Choose four speakers to present each side of the argument for and against homework. It is important that they should be able to present arguments, whether they actually agree with them or not. The four sit at the front and decide who should speak first.

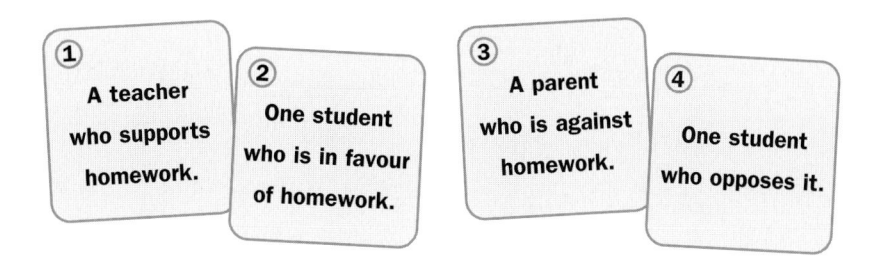

1. A teacher who supports homework.
2. One student who is in favour of homework.
3. A parent who is against homework.
4. One student who opposes it.

When all the speakers have finished choose someone to lead a discussion with the whole class.

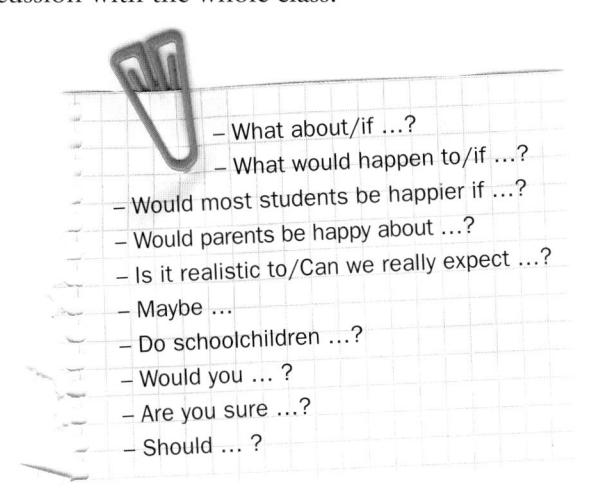

- What about/if ...?
- What would happen to/if ...?
- Would most students be happier if ...?
- Would parents be happy about ...?
- Is it realistic to/Can we really expect ...?
- Maybe ...
- Do schoolchildren ...?
- Would you ... ?
- Are you sure ...?
- Should ... ?

TIPS

1. Collect arguments for both sides of the question.
2. Take a vote to see how much support there is for each side.
3. Speakers present arguments for both sides.
4. Have a general discussion.
5. Take a second vote.

Now take another vote to see if anyone has changed their mind.

A 15 Debating / writing a poem

5. A poem about homework

This is the beginning of a poem about homework. Can you go on? Use either the words suggested or some of your own. Read your poem out to the others.

The song of the homeworkers

Homework moanwork
Cross it out and groanwork

Homework neatwork
Keeps you off the streetwork

Homework roughwork
When _____

Homework dronework
_____

Homework gloomwork
_____

Homework guesswork
_____

Homework rushwork
_____

Homework hatework
_____

Homework moanwork
Cross it out and groan groan GROANWORK.

Millum, Trevor: *The song of the homeworkers*.

Suggested words (right side):
- Gaze around the roomwork
- Book is in a messwork
- Do it on your ownwork
- Hand your book in latework
- you've had enoughwork
- Do it on the buswork

Understanding an explanatory text / summarising non-fiction — A 16

1. Test your memory

A good memory can make life much easier. How good is yours?			
Circle the number which comes closest to yourself: ① if the statement is definitely true for you ② if it is sometimes true or you are not quite sure ③ if this is never the case.			
1. I often cannot remember what a book was about just after I have read it.	1	2	3
2. Sometimes I cannot remember what a television programme was about a few minutes after it has finished.	1	2	3
3. I forget people's birthdays if I do not write them down.	1	2	3
4. If I do not write down the things I have to do I forget them.	1	2	3
5. I have sometimes completely forgotten about things I was supposed to do.	1	2	3
6. If someone gave me their phone number I could not remember it without writing it down.	1	2	3
7. It takes me a long time to learn new words in a foreign language.	1	2	3
8. I often forget to take important things to school, like books or homework.	1	2	3
9. I am always losing things.	1	2	3
10. I never know what I have spent all my money on.	1	2	3

➡ *Your score:*

No matter what your score is – borrow some books on memory training from the library.

mostly 1: Your memory seems to be causing you some problems. Try writing things down as reminders. You could improve your memory by training it.

mostly 2: Your memory seems to be fairly good, but learning a few techniques would improve it.

mostly 3: You have a good memory. You hardly ever forget things, probably because you are well organised. You have a good start, but can improve your memory even more by training.

2. Find out more about your memory

Read the following article which explains how your memory and your brain work. Read it carefully because later you will be asked to talk about it – from memory!

How our memory works

MEMORY is the ability to store and recall[1] information, observations and sensations[2]. When the brain records a new impression it transfers it firstly into the so-called 'short-term memory' then into the 'long-term' one. Whereas the contents of the short-term memory are forgotten relatively quickly, those in the long-term one can last for many years. It is the short-term memory which is most likely to be damaged by accidents, illness or drugs. The long-term one, by contrast, is much more resistant.

SOMETIMES we believe we have forgotten something and that it is lost forever. However, this is not usually the case. A bad memory is more likely to be caused by problems in recalling things rather than failing to record them in the first place. This is shown by the fact that we can suddenly remember an event which happened years ago. An enormous amount of information is locked away in our memory, all we have to do is find the key.

THERE are four traditional theories about why we forget things. One is that memories gradually fade[3] as a result of organic processes occurring[4] in the brain. Another is that in time memories become distorted[5] or changed. A third possibility is that new learning often interferes with[6] or replaces the old. Finally, some things may be forgotten because of emotional needs, for instance when unpleasant childhood experiences are repressed[7] or denied[8]. Interestingly, the ability to recall events is often connected to the feelings which accompanied[9] them. Whilst we easily forget boring things, we usually have no trouble remembering those which had a strong impact on our lives.

A 16 Understanding an explanatory text / summarising non-fiction

WHEN we take in new information it is stored in the millions of cells which make up the brain. These cells are connected by a huge network of pathways. Learning new things does not mean that the brain gradually becomes full, instead it simply creates more paths to cope with[10] the additional material.

WE are all different in the way we like information to be presented. Some people need visual material, such as pictures, diagrams and written texts, others prefer information to be presented orally and some learn best by using their sense of touch or by doing things. The senses – sight, sound, touch, taste and smell – all play a vital[11] role in our learning processes. This is illustrated by the fact that memories of past experiences are often associated with familiar smells or tastes rather than words.

ALTHOUGH the brain stores things automatically, we ourselves can also do quite a lot to improve our memories. The technique of mnemonics, for example, helps us to remember facts by means of association. For instance, it is easier to remember a shopping list if we make up a story in which the various items[12] appear.

Vocabulary: 1 *to recall* – to remember; 2 *sensation* – feeling; 3 *to fade* – to become weaker; 4 *to occur* – to happen; 5 *to become distorted* – to lose the original shape, to seem strange; 6 *to interfere with sth.* – to have a negative effect on sth.; 7 *to repress sth.* – to hide sth.; 8 *to deny sth.* – to pretend sth. does not exist; 9 *to accompany sth.* – to happen at the same time; 10 *to cope with* – to handle, deal with; 11 *vital* – extremely important; 12 *item* – article in a list

Check your understanding and your memory:

Write down five questions about the memory and brain which are answered in the article. Then cover the text up and take it in turns to ask your partner one of the questions. Answer in your own words.

3. Making notes

Read the article again, then cover it up and put the most important points into a mind map like this. Use your own words.

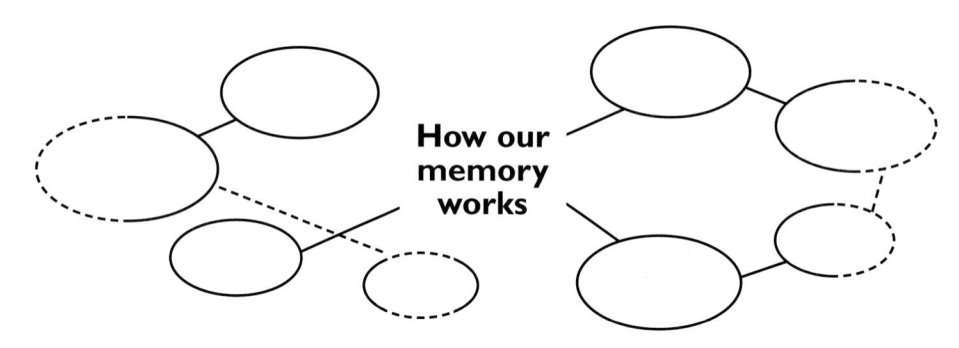

4. Writing summaries

Pick out some expressions from the article which are useful for linking ideas and explaining things, e.g.:

– linking: *whereas*
– explanations: *this is shown by ...*

Use your notes to write a summary of the article, without looking at it again.

TIPS
- Use the present tenses.
- Write in an impersonal, formal style. Do not give any personal opinions or ideas.
- Introduce the subject (e.g. *This article explains/describes ...*)
- Stick to the most important points.
- Link the ideas clearly.
- Do not end abruptly. Finish with a comment or conclusion.
- Read through your work. Check the grammar and spelling.

Understanding a literary text / summarising fiction — A17

1. Science fiction

This extract is from a science fiction story by the Russian born US author Isaac Asimov (1920–92). It was written in 1957, but takes place 200 years later. Read the whole story, silently. Try to guess any words you do not know.

Margie even wrote about it that night in her diary. On the page headed May 17, 2155, she wrote, 'Today Tommy found a real book!'

It was a very old book. Margie's grandfather once said that when he was a little boy his grandfather told him that there was a time when all stories were printed on paper.

They turned the pages, which were yellow and crinkly[1], and it was awfully funny to read words that stood still instead of moving the way they were supposed to – on a screen, you know. And then, when they turned back to the page before, it had the same words on it as it had had when they read it the first time.

'Gee,' said Tommy, 'what a waste. When you're through with[2] the book, you just throw it away, I guess. Our television screen must have had a million books on it and it's good for plenty more. I wouldn't throw that away.'

'Same with mine,' said Margie. She was eleven and hadn't seen as many telebooks as Tommy had. He was thirteen.

She said, 'where did you find it?'

'In my house.' He pointed without looking, because he was busy reading. 'In the attic.'

'What's it about?'

'School.'

Margie was scornful. 'School? What's there to write about school? I hate school.'

Margie had always hated school, but now she hated it more than ever. The mechanical teacher had been giving her test after test in geography and she had been doing worse and worse until her mother had shaken her head scornfully and sent for the County Inspector.

He was a round little man with a red face and a whole box of tools with dials[3] and wires. He smiled at her and gave her an apple, then took the teacher apart[4]. Margie had hoped he wouldn't know how to put it all together again, but he knew all right and after an hour or so, there it was again, large and black and ugly with a big screen on which all lessons were shown and the questions were asked. That wasn't so bad. The part she hated most was the slot[5] where she had to write them on a punch code[6] they made her learn when she was six years old, and the mechanical teacher calculated the mark in no time.

The inspector had smiled after he had finished and patted her head. He said to her mother, 'It's not the little girl's fault, Mrs Jones. I think the geography sector was geared[7] a little too quick. These things happen sometimes. I've slowed it up to an average ten-year level. Actually, the overall pattern of her progress is quite satisfactory.' And he patted Margie's head again.

Margie was disappointed. She had been hoping they would take the teacher away altogether. They had once taken Tommy's teacher away for nearly a month because the history sector had blanked out[8] completely.

So she said to Tommy, 'Why would anyone write about school?'

Tommy looked at her with very superior[9] eyes. 'Because it's not our kind of school, stupid. This is the old kind of school that they had hundreds and hundreds of years ago.' He added loftily[10], pronouncing the word carefully, '*Centuries* ago.'

Margie was hurt. 'Well, I don't know what kind of school they had all that time ago.' She read the book over his shoulder for a while, then said, 'Anyway, they had a teacher.'

---

1 crinkly – not flat

2 to be through with sth. (AE) – to have finished with sth.

3 dial – the face of an instrument
4 to take sth. apart – to separate sth. into the pieces which make it up
5 slot – place, *here:* window
6 punch code – code which is recorded on a card by making (punching) holes in it

7 to gear sth. – to make sth. work in a certain way

8 to blank out – to show an empty computer screen
9 superior – showing you think you are better than s.o. else
10 loftily – proudly

'Sure they had a teacher, but it wasn't a *regular* teacher. It was a man.'
'A man? How could a man be a teacher?'
'Well, he just told the boys and girls things and gave them homework and asked them questions.'
'A man isn't smart enough.'
'Sure he is. My father knows as much as my teacher.'
'He can't. A man can't know as much as a teacher.'
'He knows almost as much, I bet you.'
Margie wasn't prepared to dispute[11] that. She said, 'I wouldn't want a strange man in my house to teach me.'
Tommy screamed with laughter. 'You don't know much, Margie. The teachers didn't live in the house. They had a special building and all the kids went there.'
'And all the kids learned the same thing?'
'Sure, if they were all the same age.'
'But my mother says a teacher has to be adjusted to fit the mind of each boy and girl it teaches and that each kid has to be taught differently.'
'Just the same, they didn't do it that way then. If you don't like it, you don't have to read the book.'
'I didn't say I didn't like it,' Margie said quickly. She wanted to read about those funny schools.
They weren't even half finished when Margie's mother called, 'Margie! School!'
Margie looked up. 'Not yet, mamma.'
'Now,' said Mrs Jones. 'And it's probably time for Tommy, too.'
Margie said to Tommy, 'Can I read the book some more with you after school?'
'Maybe,' he said nonchalantly[12]. He walked away whistling[13], the dusty book tucked[14] beneath his arm.
Margie went into the schoolroom. It was right next to her bedroom, and the mechanical teacher was on and waiting for her. It was always on at the same time every day except Saturday and Sunday, because her mother said little girls learned better if they learned at regular hours.
The screen was lit up, and it said, 'Today's arithmetic lesson is on the addition of proper fractions[15]. Please insert yesterday's homework in the proper slot.'
Margie did so with a sigh. She was thinking about the old schools they had when her grandfather's grandfather was a little boy. All the kids from the whole neighbourhood came, laughing and shouting in the school yard, sitting together in the classroom, going home together at the end of the day. They learned the same things so they could help one another with the homework and talk about it.
And the teachers were people.
The mechanical teacher was flashing on the screen, 'When we add the fractions ½ and ½ …'
Margie was thinking about how the kids must have loved it in the old days. She was thinking about the fun they had.

The Fun They Had by Isaac Asimov, Liepmann AG, Zürich.

11 *to dispute sth.* – to argue about, question sth.

12 *nonchalantly* – trying to seem uninterested
13 *to whistle* – pfeifen
14 *to tuck sth. under one's arm* – to hold sth. under the arm so it does not fall out

15 *proper fraction* – German: echter Bruch

2. Starting a summary

Write a summary of lines 1–5. Imagine you are writing for someone who has not read the text. Take it in turns to read the summaries out to a partner. Suggest improvements.

TIPS
- Read the whole text to get a general idea of the contents.
- Explain the context (setting, characters, events).
- Verbalise the characters' feelings and attitudes.

3. Summarising conversations

Summarise lines 6–21 and read your work out to your partner.

TIPS
To summarise conversations:
- Do not use direct speech, report it using verbs like *ask, tell, explain, wonder, suppose*.
- Verbalise the speakers' feelings and attitudes (*be surprised, cannot understand ...*)

4. Writing a correct summary

Read this summary of lines 22–67 and correct the mistakes.

> Margie cannot understand how anyone could write about school. She hates school, except geography. Recently an inspector came and took the mechanical geography teacher out of her machine.
> Tommy explains to her that the school described in the book is the kind which existed centuries ago. Margie is hurt because he wants to read the book instead of talking to her. She wonders why the school had a man as a teacher, not a machine. She thinks men are not clever enough. Tommy laughs at her because she does not know anything about the old type of school, for instance that there was a special building for it. Margie does not believe him when he tells her that children of the same age used to learn the same thing.

Working in pairs or groups give an oral summary of the rest of the extract: the first person begins (one sentence), the next adds one more sentence and so on. Then try to reduce your summary to the most important points. Write your results down and compare them.

5. Thinking about the story

Asimov is suggesting that sometime in the future teachers will be replaced by computers and that students will learn at home. List the advantages and disadvantages of being taught this way. Could all the subjects be taught like this? Which aspects of your schooling could not be covered?

TIPS
Summarising literary texts:
- Explain the setting (who the characters are; when and where the story takes place).
- Describe the main events.
- Only interpret the events if you are asked to.

A 18 Understanding descriptive techniques / describing physical appearance

1. Describing people's appearance

List as many adjectives as you can in five minutes to describe people's physical appearance.

handsome — long
slim — fashionable

TIP
To describe people think of their height, shape, face, hair, clothes, hands, way of moving and walking.

Think of someone everyone in the class knows, for instance a classmate or a famous person. Describe their appearance in such detail that the others can guess who you are thinking of.

2. Contrasting appearances

Read this description of two men. Then make two lists of words describing the appearance of each one.

> They had walked in single file[1] down the path, and even in the open one stayed behind the other. Both were dressed in denim[2] trousers and in denim coats with brass buttons. Both wore black, shapeless hats and both carried tight blanket rolls slung over their shoulders. The first man was small and quick, dark of face, with restless eyes and sharp, strong features. Every part of him was defined[3]: small strong hands, slender arms, a thin and bony nose. Behind him walked his opposite, a huge man, shapeless of face, with large, pale eyes, with wide, sloping[4] shoulders; and he walked heavily, dragging his feet a little, the way a bear drags his paws. His arms did not swing at his sides, but hung loosely and only moved because the heavy hands were pendula[5].
>
> Steinbeck John: *Of Mice and Men*. Heinemann, p.66.

1 *in single file* – one behind the other
2 *denim* – material used for jeans

3 *defined* – clear

4 *to slope* – to have one side higher than the other

5 *pendula* – sth. heavy which swings

- size, general appearance of body?
- movements?
- features?
- hands and arms?

How does the author help us to imagine the way the second man walks?

Explain the effect of describing the two men as opposites. What else do we want to know about them?

Understanding descriptive techniques / describing physical appearance A18

3. Appearance and personality

Have you ever seen a woman with an uglier face than that? I doubt it.

But the funny thing is that Mrs Twit[1] wasn't born ugly. She'd had quite a nice face when she was young. The ugliness had grown upon her year by year as she got older.

Why would that happen? I'll tell you why.

If a person has ugly thoughts, it begins to show on the face. And when that person has ugly thoughts every day, every week, every year, the face gets uglier and uglier until it gets so ugly you can hardly bear[2] to look at it.

A person who has good thoughts cannot ever be ugly.

You can have a wonky[3] nose and a crooked[4] mouth and a double chin and stick-out teeth, but if you have good thoughts they will shine out of your face like sunbeams and you will always look lovely.

Nothing shone out of Mrs Twit's face.

In her right hand she carried a walking-stick. She used to tell people this was because she had warts growing on the sole of her left foot and walking was painful. But the real reason she carried a stick was so that she could hit things with it, things like dogs and cats and small children.

Dahl, Roald: *The Twits*. Penguin.

Vocabulary: 1 *Twit* – a twit is a silly person; 2 *to (be able to) bear to do sth.* – to be able to accept and deal with sth. unpleasant; 3 *wonky* (coll.) – bent, not straight; 4 *crooked* – curved, not straight

---

The door opened silently, and I was looking at a tall blond man in a white flannel suit with a violet satin scarf around his neck.

There was a cornflower in the lapel[1] of his white coat and his pale blue eyes looked faded out[2] by comparison. The violet scarf was loose enough to show that he wore no tie and that he had a thick, soft brown neck, like the neck of a strong woman. His features[3] were a little on the heavy side, but handsome; he had an inch more of height than I had, which made him six feet one. His blond hair was arranged, by art or nature, in three precise blond ledges[4] which reminded me of steps, so that I didn't like them. I wouldn't have liked them anyway. Apart from all this he had the general appearance of a lad who would wear a white flannel suit with a violet scarf round his neck and a cornflower in his lapel.

Chandler, Raymond: *Farewell, My Lovely* (Hamish Hamilton, 1940) Copyright 1940 by Raymond Chandler.

Vocabulary: 1 *lapel* – front part of a jacket which is folded back; 2 *faded out* – pale, without colour; 3 *features* – parts of the face (eyes, nose, mouth); 4 *ledge* – solid block, like a shelf

- Underline in the text by R. Dahl the parts which show how someone's appearance can express their personality.
- As you read the extract from a thriller by R. Chandler draw conclusions about the man's personality.
- Both extracts show how people's appearance reflects their personalities. Can you explain the difference in the writers' techniques?

4. Writing your own descriptions

Imagine you are writing a story. Introduce a character to your readers – a real person (someone you know), fictional (from a book, TV programme) or someone you make up. Only describe the person's physical appearance.

When you have finished read out your description to the class or your partner.

TIPS

Decide:
- Will the appearance give clues about personality?
- Will you put more emphasis on appearance or personality?
- Will you include your own feelings about the person or not?
- Start by making notes, putting your ideas down in any order.

A19 Direct and indirect characterisation / continuing a story

1. Direct characterisation

Read this extract and try to imagine Mr Hazell.

> Mr Victor Hazell was a brewer of beer and he owned a huge brewery. He was rich beyond words, and his property[1] stretched for miles along either side of the valley. All the land around us belonged to him, everything on both sides of the road, everything except the small patch of ground on which our filling station[2] stood. That patch belonged to my father. It was our little island in the middle of the vast ocean of Mr Hazell's estate[3].
>
> Mr Victor Hazell was a roaring[4] snob and he tried desperately to get in with[5] what he believed were the right kind of people. He hunted with the hounds and gave shooting parties and wore fancy waistcoats. Every weekday he drove his enormous silver Rolls-Royce past our filling station on his way to the brewery. As he flashed by we would sometimes catch a glimpse of[6] the great glistening[7] beery face above the wheel, pink as a ham, all soft and inflamed from drinking too much beer.
>
> Dahl, Roald: *Danny, the Champion of the World*. Penguin.

1 *property* – land and buildings
2 *filling station* – garage
3 *estate* – large area of land owned by one person or family
4 *roaring* – great
5 *to get in with* – to become friendly with
6 *to catch a glimpse of* – to see for a few seconds
7 *glistening* – shining

TIPS
- Sometimes writers directly tell us what their characters are like.
- To describe them you can use the author's own words.

Pick out words which tell us what Mr Hazell is like. Give your evidence.

Mr Hazell's personality	Evidence

Try to imagine Mr Hazell. Think about the way he might behave in everyday situations. What else do you think he does? What about his family? Write down a few ideas and compare them.

2. Use your imagination

Draw a map of the countryside described in the extract.

Can you imagine what the relationship between Mr Hazell, the father and his son is like? Write a few notes to describe this relationship and to show how the story might develop.

Mr Hazell might want to …

The boy's father might react by …

The boy …

3. Me and my kind of people

> I am a poor meek[1] thing, Mary thought, and I like quiet, meek, gentle people like myself. I liked, I *loved*, my grandmother who treated men's and women's feelings as if they were made of brittle[2] glass and who handled them with fine dextrous[3] fingers. I like people who go slowly and feel their way and are discreet and careful of their words, people who move delicately and tread on no one's dreams. 'Civilised' is my favourite word.
>
> Rendell, Ruth: *The Key to the Street.* Arrow, 1997, p.121.

1 *meek* – quiet, gentle, always willing to do what others ask
2 *brittle* – hard but breaks easily
3 *dextrous* – skilful

Are you like Mary? Do you like the same kind of people as she does? Or are you different?

Describe yourself and your kind of people.

I like … people

I like people who …

4. Indirect characterisation

> He was alone.
> His name was Terry Anders. He was fourteen years old, living in Cleveland, Ohio, and his parents had left him.
> Of course it didn't happen quite that suddenly. The first call came at almost exactly eight o'clock. His mother called first.
> 'Terry, I'm not coming home. I can't take it any longer. I've taken all my things. Tell your father I won't be there to fight him any longer. You'll both have to do without me.' And she hung up.
> He had said almost nothing. Had once more felt a sense of wonder – this time at why he didn't seem to care all that much that his mother had gone. A part of him felt bad, but it was mostly because he *didn't* feel bad that he felt bad. She was gone – that thought was there – and there wouldn't be any more fights.
> His father called just after nine.
> 'Tell your mother I'm not coming back – I've got all my stuff. I'm sick of the whole thing.' And he hung up.
> Terry put the phone back and looked out the window at the road in the darkness and thought: So, they aren't going to be here. Neither one. At least for a little while Mother thinks I'm staying here with Father and Father thinks I'm staying here with Mother.
> I'm alone.
> Just me.
> And the house.
> Oh yes, he thought, and a smile came, widened into a grin. There's one thing.
> The car.
>
> Paulsen, Gary: *The Car.* Hamish Hamilton, 1994.

a) Explain how Terry feels about his mother leaving home.
b) How do we get to know Terry? What technique does the writer use?
c) Look at the way the words are written down at the end when we learn about Terry's feelings. Can you imagine why the writer arranged them in this way?

What do you think Terry will do next? What would you do?

TIPS
- Sometimes writers describe their characters indirectly, by showing their behaviour and thoughts.
- To interpret these characters you have to draw your own conclusions.

A 20 Characterisation through dialogue / writing dialogue

1. A conversation between two schoolgirls

Read this scene from a play in which two 14-year-old girls, Claire and Paula, have to take part in a school race organised by their teacher, Miss Dunn. The girls are standing behind some flags, ready to start. Try to guess the meanings of any new words. Are there any words you cannot guess?

Miss Dunn:	Right girls. Everyone line up behind the flags, please. *(Crowded commotion)* Don't push. Spread yourselves right down the track.
Helen:	Not fair, miss. The ones at the front get a start on us.
Miss Dunn:	It's four miles, Helen. I'm sure you'll catch up.
Claire:	*(Mimicking)* Not fair, miss.
Paula:	I don't see why everybody has to run. Why don't they just let the Helen Clarks an' them get on with it. They'll win anyway. We could just stay and cheer.
Claire:	Wouldn't cheer that stuck-up thing.
Miss Dunn:	Claire Morton! What are you doing with your coat on?
Claire:	It's freeezing, miss.
Miss Dunn:	Don't be stupid. You can't run in that.
Claire:	Don't want to run.
Miss Dunn:	Take it off.
Claire:	Nowhere to put it.
Miss Dunn:	Give it here. Get into line. You too, Paula Wood. *(Calling)* Everybody ready? *(Gun fires. A stampede)*
Claire:	*(Running)* Hang on, Paula. Don't run so rotten fast.
Paula:	I'm getting carried away with the rest.
Claire:	We'll be carried off if we keep this pace up. Four miles and we're not out of the gate yet.
Paula:	Helen Clark is.
Claire:	Slow down.
Paula:	We're last now.
Claire:	Good. That way nobody'll see us skiving off.
Paula:	How d'you mean?
Claire:	My house is just round the corner. Let's nip in there for a cup of tea.
Paula:	We can't do that. We'll be miles behind.
Claire:	They come back the same way, stupid. We'll just tuck in behind them. Nobody'll know.
Paula:	I don't …
Claire:	What's the problem?
Paula:	I don't want people calling me a cheat …
Claire:	They won't know. Anyway, it's not as if we're trying to win. We're going to be last in any case, so what's the diff… Come on, if you're that keen on running I'll race you to my house.
	(Claire's kitchen)
Claire:	Want a top-up?
Paula:	Thanks.
Claire:	There's some chocolate biscuits in that tin.
Paula:	Shouldn't really but … go on, then. What sort do you want? Marathon?

Williams, David: Skivers. In: Foster, T. (ed.): *Sport.* Oxford University Press, 1997.

Characterisation through dialogue / writing dialogue **A 20**

2. Style

Look at the way the girls speak and suggest the writer's reasons for choosing this style. Give examples.

TIP

To interpret characters in drama think about what they say and their way (style) of speaking.

3. Dialogue reveals character

The scene gives us some clues as to the girls' personalities. If you were writing about them how would you develop each character? Pick out some of these words to describe each girl. You can add more.

adventurous	cautious	cheeky	conscientious	co-operative	dishonest
disobedient	domineering	egoistic	fun-loving	hardworking	honest
imaginative	impulsive	independent	lively	obedient	open
peace-loving	polite	popular	quiet	respectful	responsible
self-confident	serious	slow to show feelings	timid	tough	well-behaved

What do you think the girls look like? Try to sketch them.
Add hair and clothes.

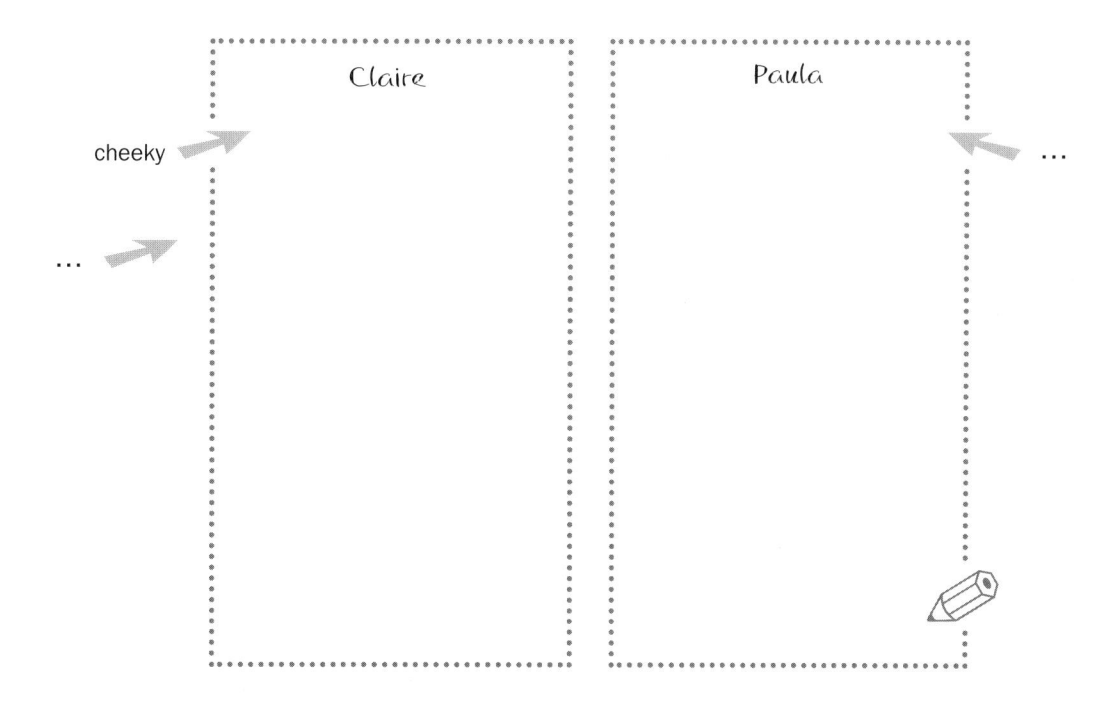

Claire   Paula

cheeky →   ← ...

... →

4. What next?

Claire and Paula run back to school, but get the timing wrong and arrive before the rest. What do you think happens next? In groups write out a conversation either between the two girls and their teacher or between Claire and Paula and the rest of the class.

A 21 Humour through taking things literally

1. An unusual meeting

This is an extract from the famous children's classic 'Alice in Wonderland', which is also enjoyed by many adults. Read it and try to guess any words you do not understand.

Suggest the author's reason for writing 'cat' with a capital 'C'.

What is your first impression of Alice? Support your opinion with examples.

Alice has fallen down a rabbit hole into 'Wonderland'. She is standing near a tree when she suddenly sees a cat sitting in it.

The Cat only grinned when it saw Alice. It looked good-natured, she thought: still it had very long claws and a great many teeth, so she felt that it ought to be treated with respect.

'Cheshire Puss,'[1] she began, rather timidly, as she did not at all know whether it would like the name: however, it only grinned a little wider. 'Come, it's pleased so far,' thought Alice, and she went on. 'Would you tell me, please, which way I ought to go from here?'

'That depends a good deal[2] on where you want to get to,' said the Cat.

'I don't much care where …' said Alice.

'Then it doesn't matter which way you go,' said the Cat.

'… so long as I get *somewhere*,' Alice added as an explanation.

'Oh, you're sure to do that,' said the Cat, 'if you only walk long enough.'

Alice felt that this could not be denied, so she tried another question. 'What sort of people live about here?'

'In *that* direction,' the Cat said, waving its right paw round, 'lives a Hatter: and in *that* direction,' waving the other paw, 'lives a March Hare. Visit either you like: they're both mad.'[3]

'But I don't want to go among mad people,' Alice remarked.

'Oh, you can't help that,' said the Cat: 'we're all mad here. I'm mad. You're mad.'

'How do you know I'm mad?' said Alice.

'You must be,' said the Cat, 'or you wouldn't have come here.'

Alice didn't think that proved it at all: however, she went on: 'And how do you know that you're mad?'

'To begin with,' said the Cat, 'a dog's not mad. You grant that?'

'I suppose so,' said Alice.

'Well, then,' the Cat went on, 'you see a dog growls when it's angry, and wags its tail when it's pleased. Now I growl when I'm pleased, and wag my tail when I'm angry. Therefore I'm mad.'

'*I* call it purring, not growling,' said Alice.

'Call it what you like,' said the Cat.

Carroll, Lewis: Alice's Adventures in Wonderland. In: Green, R.L.: *The Works of Lewis Carroll*. Paul Hamlyn, London, 1965, p. 65.

Vocabulary:
1. A *Cheshire cat* is a certain type of cat (*Cheshire* is also the name of an English county); *puss* or *pussy (cat)* is a word used by children meaning 'cat'
2. *a good deal* – quite a bit
3. *Hatter, March Hare* – there are two idioms, 'as mad as a hatter' and 'as mad as a March hare' (in March, the breeding season, hares are unusually wild)

2. Thinking about humour

How do you think Alice expected the Cat to reply to her request for help? Explain why its responses to her request for help are funny.

Can you see a more serious point to the Cat's behaviour?

3. Who is mad?

Alice tries to start a polite conversation by asking about the sort of people who live in the area. Look at the Cat's replies and think about what it is really telling her. Explain how Alice finally supports the Cat's argument, possibly without wanting to.

4. The Cat's point of view

Imagine you are the Cheshire Cat. What do you think about Alice?

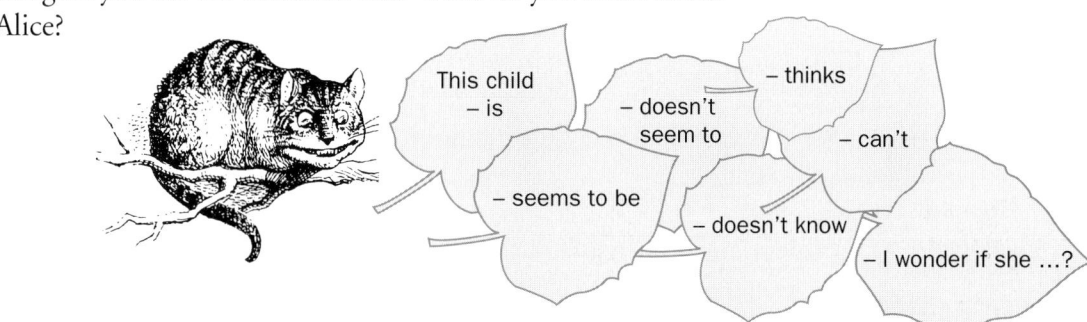

- This child – is
- – doesn't seem to
- – thinks
- – can't
- – seems to be
- – doesn't know
- – I wonder if she …?

5. Taking things literally

The Cat always gives people unexpected answers. Can you pick out its replies to each of these questions?

A. As little as possible.
B. No, it's too high.
C. Go on a diet.
D. Yes, run.
E. No one. I had to fight for it.
F. Yes.
G. No, but give me time and I will.

1. Excuse me, do you know the quickest way to the town hall?
2. Excuse me, do you know the time?
3. Who gave you that black eye?
4. Have you forgotten that you owe me five pounds?
5. What do you do for a living?
6. Can you stand on your head?
7. What are you going to do when you're as big as your mother?

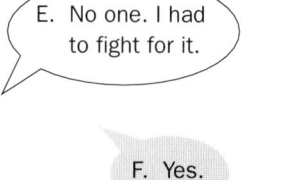

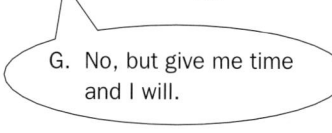

In groups take it in turns to read out these questions. The others should try to think of funny replies.

A teacher asks:
1. How can you make so many mistakes in one day?
2. I've had to punish you every day this week, Brian. What have you got to say?
3. I asked you to write an essay on cheese last night.
4. I hope I didn't see you looking at Susan's exam paper, Tony?
5. If I had six apples and wanted to divide them between eight children, how would I do it?
6. If your father knew how badly you've behaved, Johnny, he'd get grey hair overnight.
7. We start school at nine.
8. Which part of going to school do you like best?

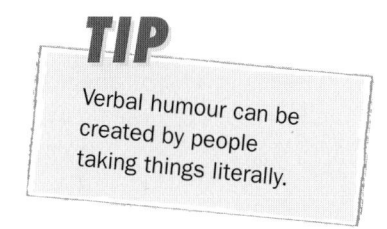

TIP
Verbal humour can be created by people taking things literally.

A 22 Humorous poems: nonsense, puns / writing poetry

1. A nonsense poem

Explain the contradictions in this nonsense poem.
(You can't … If you …)

> I went to the pictures tomorrow.
> I took a front seat at the back.
> I fell from the pit[1] to the gallery[2]
> And broke a front bone in my back.
> A lady gave me some chocolate,
> I ate it and gave it her back.
> I phoned for a taxi and walked home
> And that's why I never came back.

1 *pit* – the seats in the bottom part of a theatre
2 *gallery* – the highest seats in a theatre

Correct the poem so it is more logical. It does not matter if it no longer rhymes.
In groups or with a partner try to make up a nonsense poem of your own.

2. Playing with words

Read this poem aloud to yourself. Do you understand the humour?

POTATO CLOCK

A potato clock, a potato clock
    Has anybody got a potato clock?
A potato clock, a potato clock
    Oh where can I find a potato clock?

I went down to London the other day
Found myself a job with a lot of pay
Carrying bricks on a building site
From early in the morning till late at night.

No one here works as hard as me
I never even break for a cup of tea
My only weakness, my only crime
Is that I never get to work on time.

I arrived this morning half an hour late
The foreman came up in a terrible state
'You've got a good job, but you'll lose it, cock*,
If you don't get up at eight o'clock.'

Up at eight o'clock, up at eight o'clock
    Has anybody got up at eight o'clock?
Up at eight o'clock, up at eight o'clock
    Oh where can I find up at eight o'clock?

A potato clock, a potato clock
    Has anybody got a potato clock?
A potato clock, a potato clock
    Oh where can I find a potato clock?

*cock – a slang word for 'friend, man'

Reprinted by permission of PFD on behalf of: Roger McGough
© Roger McGough: Potato clock. In: McGough, R.: *Sky in the Pie*. Kestrel Books, 1983.

Humorous poems: nonsense, puns / writing poetry **A 22**

3. Recognising puns

The humour in this poem comes from the double meanings of many words, also known as puns. Pick them out and explain them. Your dictionary will help.

Have you ever seen?

Have you ever seen a sheet on a river bed?
Or a single hair from a hammer's head?
Has the foot of a mountain any toes?
And is there a pair of garden hose¹?
Does the needle ever wink its eye?
Why doesn't the wing of a building fly?

Can you tickle the ribs of a parasol?
Or open the trunk of a tree at all?
Are the teeth of a rake ever going to bite?
Have the hands of a clock any left or right?
Can the garden plot² be deep and dark?
And what is the sound of the birch's bark?

(Anonymous)

Vocabulary: 1 *hose* – old-fashioned word for 'trousers'; 2 *plot* – piece of land

Now read the poem again just to enjoy it.

TIP
Don't miss any humour. Look out for plays on words – the sounds or double meanings.

4. Writing your own poem

How many excuses can you think of for not doing your homework? Write a poem about it. The lines do not need to rhyme.

Where's your homework?

Smith! Where's your homework?
The dog ate it, Sir.
Oh, ok do it again then.

Poulter! Where's your homework?
_____ Sir.
Oh, ok do it again then.

Rudd! Where's your homework?
_____ Sir.
Oh, ok do it again then.

Rendell! Where's your homework?
Here it is, Sir.
But this is a blank sheet of paper!
_____ Sir.
Oh, ok good lad.

Sexton! Where's your homework?
I haven't done it, Sir.
Why haven't you done it?
Because I watched T.V. instead, Sir.
Do you expect me to believe
Such a stupid excuse, boy?

Walsh, Gez: *Someone's Nicked my Knickers*. Rotherham: The King's England Press 1999, p.19

A 23 Irony and euphemisms in a fable

1. A fable

Read this fable and try to guess any new words.

> ### The rabbits who caused all the trouble
>
> Within the memory of the youngest child there was a family of rabbits who lived near a pack of wolves. The wolves announced that they did not like the way the rabbits were living. (The wolves were crazy about the way they themselves were living, because it was the only way to live.) One night several wolves were killed in an earthquake and this was blamed on the rabbits, for it is well known that rabbits pound on the ground with their hind legs and cause earthquakes. On another night one of the wolves was killed by a bolt of lightning and this was also blamed on the rabbits, for it is well known that lettuce-eaters cause lightning. The wolves threatened to civilize the rabbits if they didn't behave, and the rabbits decided to run away to a desert island. But the other animals, who lived at a great distance, shamed them, saying, "You must stay where you are and be brave. This is no world for escapists. If the wolves attack you, we will come to your aid, in all probability." So the rabbits continued to live near the wolves and one day there was a terrible flood which drowned a great many wolves. This was blamed on the rabbits for it is well known that carrot-nibblers with long ears cause floods. The wolves descended on the rabbits, for their own good, and imprisoned them in a dark cave, for their own protection.
>
> When nothing was heard about the rabbits for some weeks, the other animals demanded to know what had happened to them. The wolves replied that the rabbits had been eaten and since they had been eaten the affair was a purely internal matter. But the other animals warned that they might possibly unite against the wolves unless some reason was given for the destruction of the rabbits. So the wolves gave them one. "They were trying to escape," said the wolves, "and, as you know, this is no world for escapists."
>
> Thurber, James: The rabbits who caused all the trouble. From: *Fables for our time* by James Thurber (Hamish Hamilton, 1939). Copyright © James Thurber, 1951.

List the reasons the wolves give for disliking the rabbits.
How do you react to the story-teller's (narrator's) attitude to these arguments?
Do you see, now, how the title should be interpreted?

2. Misusing language to disguise the truth

This quotation from the famous children's novel *Through the Looking Glass* by Lewis Carroll illustrates the way those in power often misuse language for their own purposes:

> "When *I* use a word," Humpty Dumpty said, in a rather scornful tone, "it means just what I choose it to mean. Neither more nor less." "The question is," said Alice, "whether you can make words mean so many different things." "The question is," said Humpty Dumpty, "who is to be master. That is all."

Give examples of the way the wolves misuse language in order to exercise power over others.

Rephrase these expressions to expose their real meanings:

1. The American pioneers 'civilised' the natives
2. 'ethnic cleansing'
3. to 'liquidate' someone
4. to 'correct' borders
5. the soldiers 'took out' the rebels
6. 're-education centres'
7. to 'rationalise' the organisation of a business
8. 'adjustment to the work force'
9. 'an opportunity for a change of career'
10. a 'very physical' football player.

Irony and euphemisms in a fable — A 23

3. Irony

The powerful effect of the fable results from ironic contrasts, for instance between what the wolves say and what they do. Explain the ironic contrast produced by the narrator's style.

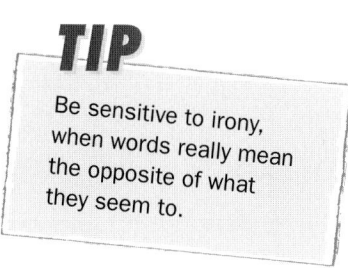

TIP
Be sensitive to irony, when words really mean the opposite of what they seem to.

4. The rabbits as scapegoats

Explain how the wolves try to build up a picture of the rabbits as the enemy.
Suggest why scapegoats can be useful to those in power in any society.

5. The other animals

Work with a partner. Your partner is one of the other animals and you are a visitor. The rabbits have been killed. Ask your partner to explain the behaviour of the others towards the rabbits. Then exchange roles.

YOU
- Why did/didn't ...?
- But you could have ...
- Couldn't you have ...?
- Didn't/Can't you see ...?
- Haven't you learned ...?
- Do you always ...?

YOUR PARTNER
- What could we have ...?
- We thought/were ...
- We didn't know/understand ...
- How could we know that ...?
- But we've been taught to ...
- We need someone to ...

6. The allegory

Although most fables seem to be about animals they are really comments on human society. Decide what kind of people the animals in Thurber's fable represent.

Which of the animals do you think the fable is criticising most? Translate this into human behaviour and explain the warnings to the readers.

Do you see any wider significance in the wolves' statement that what happened to the rabbits was 'a purely internal matter'?

TIP
Be aware of hidden, allegorical meanings, especially, but not only, in fables.

7. The moral

The aim of a fable is to teach us a lesson about life. To make sure that we understand the real message a 'moral' is always added at the end.

Make up a moral of your own for Thurber's fable. Decide first who you are aiming your advice at, the rabbits or the others.

A 24 Writing the ending to a short story / changing the point of view

1. Interpreting a short story

Read this story through once to get a general idea of the contents. The ending is missing.

When we dead awaken *by Ronald Duncan*

I do not think I am more avaricious[1] than most men; but the chance of obtaining something for nothing has always appealed to me. Especially when I could pick it with my own hands; blackberrries, for these I will tear my clothes to pieces, nettle my face and hands, all for the pleasure of reaching
5 the inaccessible something for nothing, and the pleasure of holding the plump[2] fruit in my fingers. So, too, with mushrooms; as a child I began the search; and as a man, with less energy but the same incentive[3], I continue it. I will walk my friends' feet off to find a few more of those will-o'-the wisp[4] delicacies; and always there is a hope in the back of my mind that I will again
10 find a complete mushroom ring, enough for a feast and to sell the rest as sheer[5] profit. Such frail[6] chances are strong ropes tethering[7] many of us to pursuits[8] and hobbies which, were we to consider the time we devote[9] to them, would prove to us that it is impossible to obtain anything for nothing. And, as my wife has often reminded me, there is little profit in obtaining
15 three pounds of wild fruit at the cost of a torn shirt and a large cleaning bill.

    I knew every inch of the way and was soon scaling[10] the precipitous[11] surface which, being dry, seemed safe even to my nervous eye. Gulls[12] scissored the air and sliced the sky and then would stay poised[13] and then fall and then rise. I kept my eyes to the rock and felt like a wood louse invading their
20 pinnacle[14] of a home. The top of the rock was relatively flat. I climbed on to my feet and eyed the ground for the precious eggs. To my disappointment I found only three where I had expected at least three dozen, though I saw scores of clumsily built, empty nests littered[16] with the husks[17] of my own seed corn. I could not allow myself to return with only three eggs, for there
25 would be six of us to luncheon and I promised my wife that I could provide the *pièce de résistance*[18] for that meal. On descending the rock I noticed that a great number of gulls circled a ledge of the main cliff some hundred feet above me. It was there, I supposed, that a friend of mine went for his eggs; for he always returned with a full basket and sold them for sixty pence a
30 dozen, something for nothing. The cliff looked easy, that is, as easy as the rock I had already climbed. So, with my basket in my teeth, I began the ascent[19]. Within ten mintes I was at the top, my basket full, it had been easy. I smoked a cigarette and admired the view, meditating on the pleasure the eggs would give my wife and wondering whether she would be able to pre-
35 serve some for the winter. I had two pounds' worth of eggs; something for nothing, I was happy. I picked up my basket and then looked for my way down. But I could not see how I had managed to climb to where I now stood. I stood on a ledge of cliff four feet wide; at the back of me was an overhanging precipitous cliff which I knew it was impossible to scale. And each
40 side of me a sheer[20] drop of one hundred feet with the rocks and the sea's snarl[21] at the bottom. In front, the ledge narrowed till it was a foot wide – no more than a plank – and on each side a sheer drop with nothing to hold on to.

    Instantly, as though pricked[22] by a hypodermic syringe[23], sharp panic
45 spread over me and the sick fear of what lay before me settled[24] in my throat as I realized what I had done. I had walked this narrow ledge, this one-foot plank, without noticing it, with my eyes searching for something for nothing; I had managed to keep my balance over nothing. But now it was a different matter. My nerve had gone. I could not even stand where the ledge was com-
50 paratively wide. So I crawled inch by inch to where it narrowed and peered[25]

1 *avaricious* – greedy
2 *plump* – fat
3 *incentive* – wish, desire
4 *will-o'-the wisp* – sth. almost impossible to get
5 *sheer* – *here:* total, complete
6 *frail* – weak, delicate, slight
7 *to tether* – to tie (an animal)
8 *pursuit* – interest, activity
9 *to devote (sth./o.s. to sth./s.o.)* – to give one's time and energy to s.o./sth.
10 *to scale* – to climb up sth. steep (wall, cliff)
11 *precipitous* – high, dangerous
12 *gull* – German: Möwe
13 *to poise* – to balance in one position
14 *pinnacle* – highest point
15 *scores* – lots
16 *littered* – covered with rubbish
17 *husk* – outer covering
18 *pièce de résistance* – the most important or impressive part

19 *ascent* – way upwards, climb

20 *sheer* – *here:* very steep
21 *to snarl* – (dogs) to show the teeth and growl angrily
22 *to prick* – to make a very small hole in sth. with a sharp point
23 *hypodermic syringe* – German: Spritze
24 *to settle* – *here:* to establish itself, grow
25 *to peer* – to look carefully

Writing the ending to a short story / changing the point of view — A 24

over. Each side was a sheer descent of slate[26]-smooth rock. The ledge was less than a foot wide and more than five yards long. I must have crossed this without noticing it.

I knew I could not do it again.

55 I knew that I must do it again.

There was no other way, no other alternative. If only I could regain my nerve. I lit another cigarette and I lay flat out, my hand holding a crack in the rock. My only chance was to make a run for it, with my eyes on some distant point, some imagined gull's nest. It could soon be over and, when it was, 60 I swore in my panic to keep so many resolutions[27]. I thought of my wife waiting for the eggs, and our laughing over my present predicament[28]. Standing up, I threw my cigarette away and, with my eyes on a fixed point the other side, began to run towards the ledge, the sea almost meeting underneath it, the gulls swooping[29] over it. I was on the ledge, my eyes still fixed on the 65 point beyond it. In two seconds I would be across. A gull swooped towards me, my eyes lost their fixed objective, I hesitated …

Then later I found myself sitting on the beach; I do not know how long I had sat there. I cannot tell; I may have dozed[30], I may have slept. The tide may have turned[31] or the year turned[32]. I do not know. I picked up my bas-
70 ket and walked up the path from the beach to the cottage. I thought of my wife waiting, the table laid, the guests' inconsequential chatter[33].

I put my basket behind my back and opened the door. The room was empty, there was no table laid. I went upstairs still carrying the basket of eggs. My wife lay on the bed. She was sobbing[34]. I asked her what was wrong, she 75 made no reply. Sobbing, she looked away from me. I begged[35] her to tell me why she was crying. She made no answer. I put my hand out and touched her smooth, hot forehead. Instantly she screamed, rose from the bed and ran down the stairs out into the night. I followed, but could not find her. I returned to the empty house and went to my study and lay there, miserable[36] and be-
80 wildered[37].

26 *slate* – German: Schiefer

27 *resolution* – promise, decision
28 *predicament* – problem, difficult situation

29 *to swoop* – to come down quickly and suddenly

30 *to doze* – to sleep lightly
31 *to turn* (tide) – to change direction (the sea)
32 *to turn* (year) – to come to an end
33 *inconsequential chatter* – talk about unimportant things
34 *to sob* – to cry hard
35 *to beg* – to ask in a worried way

36 *miserable* – extremely unhappy
37 *bewildered* – confused

Can you imagine how the story goes on?

2. The ending

This is the original ending of the story. Compare it with your own. What is the main difference? Explain which you prefer and why.

How long I slept there I do not know. The day may have drunk the night a dozen times for all I know; but when I awoke the stream still ran by the cottage. And I listened. My study is next to the sitting-room. Through the door I could hear voices and a fire crackling[38]. It could not be the luncheon party, for we seldom light fires during May. I listened. My sister was there, she was serving coffee. My wife was there and there were two men with them; one was my neighbour, the other a friend of the family. Both people who would often drop in for an evening. I listened; my wife was no longer crying, the wireless[39] was on. I opened the door slowly and went in; my neighbour sat in my chair, so I went over to the divan[40].

Nobody looked at me, nobody spoke to me and nobody passed me any coffee. They went on talking with the music playing.

My wife looked pretty; she went on knitting. What had I done to be left unnoticed?

I stood up and went to my wife's chair and on her lap[41] placed the basket of gulls' eggs. Her eyes rose slowly from her knitting and she screamed. 'Take them away, take them away!' she screamed, and ran from the room crying. My sister followed her. Then my friend said to my neighbour: 'Poor woman, she's still unnerved[42]. That's the second time she's thought she's seen her husband carrying gulls' eggs … She must go away.'

I went into my study. So I was dead, was I? When will we dead awaken?

Duncan, Ronald: When we dead awaken. In: *Cornish Short Stories*. Penguin 1976.

38 *to crackle* – to make small, sharp sounds

39 *wireless* – radio (old-fashioned)

40 *divan* – long low seat with no back or arms

41 *lap* – part of the body between stomach and knees when s.o. is sitting

42 *unnerved* – having lost confidence because the nerves are upset

3. Clues

We are given clues about what happened to the man. Read the story again and try to pick them out.

TIP
Think while you read. Be creative, develop theories, look for clues.

4. Changing the point of view

The impact of the story is the result of the unusual point of view. Compare the difference in effect by writing it from a different angle, that of the ghost's wife.

TIP
Authors carefully choose the point of view from which to tell their stories. The interpretation of the events depends on this point of view.

Teaching notes   A1 A3

A1 Reading habits

Students are asked to reflect about their own reading habits. At the same time they are encouraged to broaden their reading.

1. Your attitudes to reading

A questionnaire helps the class to reflect about their own attitudes to reading. After each learner has filled in a questionnaire the results are compared and discussed. A class profile can be compiled, showing the most – and least – popular types of reading material. Students should try to give reasons for their choices (e.g. *to help me with my school work, just for enjoyment, to relax* etc.).

2. The things you read

Students reflect in more detail about their choices of reading material. Thinking about the sources of it (library etc.) might reveal a few more possibilities than they were previously aware of.

Think about ... Can you ...?
Possible suggestions: *Thrillers, horror stories, detective stories, adventure stories, science fiction, fantasy, myths, legends, romance, comics, magazines, newspapers, informative books, travel writing, biography, autobiography, poetry.*
Sources: *From the town/school library, home, friends, bookshop.*

3. My choice

Each student writes a brief description of a favourite book, fiction or non-fiction. These recommendations can be collected and used as a reading list, to be continually augmented.

A2 Recognising different types of texts

Students learn that good readers are able to get a general idea of a piece of writing from the first few lines because they recognise the type of text. As they read they make use of their previous knowledge of and expectations about that particular type of text.

1. Recognising different kinds of writing

Working in pairs or groups the class identify the types of texts by matching them with the descriptions.

Look at ...
Newspaper article: 2, Letter to a magazine: 4, Message or note: 1, Novel: 10, Public notice: 5, Postcard: 6, Formal letter: 7, Diary: 11, Instructions: 8, Advertisement: 3 (Although at first sight this looks like a personal letter, it is in fact an advertisement for Nokia. 'The World in 2000'.)
Film review: 9

A3 Skimming advertisements/ making telephone enquiries

A page of holiday advertisements offers practice in skimming through texts in order to get a general idea of them.

1. Looking through advertisements

Students should only be allowed a few minutes to quickly skim through the advertisements. They should not read them in detail, but rather try to get a rough idea of the contents.

Look at ...
1. What are the advertisements for? – *different types of holidays*
2. Some of the different types of holidays – *expeditions, boating, walking tours, cycling, sightseeing, adventure holidays, camping, activity holidays, rock climbing, amusement park.*
3. Pick out – Each student selects two of the adverts and explains why this particular type of holiday would interest them.
4. Which advert does not interest you at all? – Learners explain why they dislike one of the types of holiday advertised.

2. A survey

Pairs of learners take it in turns to interview each other about holiday preferences. Each person notes down their partner's answers and reports them back to the class, using the vocabulary aids provided. Later a class profile can be composed to reflect general likes and dislikes.

A3 Teaching notes
A4

3. Making enquiries

Having gained a general idea about the contents of the adverts students now read them in detail and select one which interests them. Working in pairs they make up a phone call in which one person asks for information and the other gives it. They exchange roles so that each partner practices asking for more details. The conversations can then be acted or read out in front of the class or written down.

A4 Skimming with the help of illustrations and headings / making notes (table)

Before good readers look at a text in detail they first skim through it quickly to see what it is about. Headings, subheadings and illustrations help to give a general orientation. The reading process is also more effective if any previous knowledge of the topic is activated first. This not only stimulates interest, but also facilitates the incorporation of the new information with the old.

1. Skimming for the general idea
Before you read ...
Working in pairs or groups the class note down what they already know about New York.

Then get a general ...
Students should only be allowed a few minutes to skim through the text in order to prevent them from reading it in detail. At this stage they should concentrate on getting a rough idea of the contents.

Write down ...
In pairs or groups, learners specify their expectations from the text by formulating a few questions which they think it will answer. Without reading the article in detail they suggest which parts of it might contain this information.
Possible questions:
– *When did New York begin to exist?* (→ THE BEGINNING)
– *Why did people first go to New York?* (→ THE BEGINNING)
– *What was New York like when it first began?* (→ THE BEGINNING)
– *Is New York just Manhattan?* (→ A CITY GROWS)
– *Why are there so many people of different nationalities in New York?* (→ A MULTICULTURAL CITY)
– *What is there to do in New York?* (→ THINGS TO DO)
– *What sights should you go and see?* (→ THINGS TO DO)
– *What is the best way to get around the city?* (→ GETTING AROUND)

2. Reading for detail
Learners read the whole extract silently. They then write down any answers to their questions and discuss whether any questions still remain and whether new ones have been raised.

3. Making notes
Students learn that prose information can be made more accessible for future reference if it is converted into table form. The first step in this process is to locate the most important points.

Find ...
Answers will vary, but the following might be regarded as the most important points.

> THE BEGINNING. New York, also known as the 'Big Apple', is a city which is constantly changing. It is very difficult to imagine what it was like a century ago and almost impossible to picture it when it <u>first came into existence as the trading station Nieuw Amsterdam, built by Dutch settlers in 1625</u>. The <u>name was changed to New York by the British</u>, when they captured it in <u>1664</u>.
> New York City began as a <u>sea port</u>. In those days the whole of its coastline was full of ships of all kinds – cargo boats, trans-Atlantic liners, warships, ferries, pleasure boats, police launches and fishing boats. This constant sea traffic made the waterways look like today's congested motorways. Now, when we think of New York, we do not immediately associate it with shipping. Indeed, a stranger to the

city might hardly realize that it is a port at all, since the sea is blocked out by solid walls of skyscrapers. But although shipping is no longer so important, New York still functions as a port and has the largest harbour in the US.

A CITY GROWS. New York City grew rapidly and by 1790 it was the largest city in the US with a population of about 33,000. In 1898 five districts joined together – Manhattan, Brooklyn, Queens, Bronx and Staten Island – which boosted the population to around 3.4 million. Another reason for this increase was the influx of immigrants, mostly from Europe. Between 1815 and 1914 about 35 million people emigrated to the US. From 1892–1924 the main entry point was Ellis Island in New York Bay.

A MULTICULTURAL CITY. Today New York streets are a lively mix of about 7 million mainly English-speaking Americans, whose ancestors came firstly from Europe and later Asia, South and Central America, Africa and the Pacific and Caribbean islands. During the last century the population has changed enormously from an almost all-white majority to a colourful mixture (see graph).
The influx of immigrants has been tremendously valuable to the city since they brought with them new skills and different styles of music, dress and cooking.

Further information
For more information on New York see the Internet web page www.newyork.citysearch.com.

4. The contribution of immigrants
Students become aware of the huge contribution which immigrants make to the culture of their new country. Working in groups they list some of the additions to their own culture.

Make a list …
Some suggestions:
– *Food: a wide variety of foods and ethnic restaurants. To name but a few: pizza, spaghetti, kebabs, various fruits, vegetables and spices (tomatoes, peppers, oregano, chili), different kinds of bread (baguette, pitta), tea, coffee, cocoa.*
– *Music: blues, hip-hop, jazz, reggae, rock-and-roll.*

A 5 Skimming: Reading and writing book descriptions ('blurbs')

One typical use of the skill of skimming is when we choose books to read. By looking at the cover and reading the decription or 'blurb' on the back we gain a general impression of the contents of a book.
Students practise gleaning as much information as possible in a short time by skimming through a collection of blurbs. They then use these descriptions as models for writing about a book or film which they once enjoyed.

Table:

History	Growth up to 1924	Population today
– Dutch settlers built trading station Nieuw Amsterdam, 1625. – Renamed New York by British, 1664. – Originally sea port. Still a port, but no longer so important.	– Grew rapidly, by 1790 largest city in US (33,000). – 1898 five districts joined together (Manhattan, Brooklyn, Queens, Bronx, Staten Island). Population now around 3.4 million. – Influx of immigrants, mostly European. Ellis Island.	– Ancestors from Europe, later Asia, South and Central America, Africa, Pacific and Caribbean islands. – Great changes in population, almost all-white majority to colourful mixture. – Influx of immigrants tremendously valuable.

A 5 Teaching notes
A 6

1. Choosing a book
Students are only allowed a few minutes to glance at the blurbs in order to prevent them from reading in too much detail. The activity can take the form of a competition between groups or two teams: the blurbs are covered up and the groups or teams write down the answers. Results are then compared.

Look at …
1. Which different kinds of books are described? *Novels (A, F), (children's) encyclopedias (B, H), football annual (C), funny stories (about criminals, I), how people behave (when they meet, E), how detectives work (G), jokes and cartoons (D).*
2. Are there any encyclopedias? *Yes, two, B and H.*
3. Is there a children's encyclopedia? *Yes, both of them, B and H.*
4. What is one of the novels about?
   – *An ordinary boy who finds out he is a wizard (J.K.Rowling's children's books about Harry Potter);*
   – *A one-legged fanatic who wants to kill a whale that has crippled him. (Herman Melville's 'Moby Dick').*
5. Are there any funny books? *I (stories about stupid criminals), D (collection of jokes and cartoons).*
6. One of the books is about people's behaviour in everyday life. What does it describe? *It describes the impression people make on others when they first meet (E).*
7. Are there any books about hobbies or sports? *Sports, C (football annual).*

2. Your choice
Pairs of students ask each other which book or books they would or would not like to read. They then report back to the class. A class profile could be developed to show which of the books are the most and least popular.

3. Which would you prefer?
Silently, the class reads each book description and say which book they would prefer to read, giving reasons. The extract on the left is from *Carrie*, by Stephen King, 1974. The other is from William Golding's *Lord of the Flies*, 1954.

4. My suggestion
With the help of the vocabulary aids on the worksheet learners write a description praising a book or film which they once enjoyed. The descriptions are then collected and distributed at random among the class. Students comment on the effectiveness of the descriptions, saying whether they would now like to read the book or see the film and whether there is enough detail or too much, so that the suspense is lost. The descriptions could then be collected, typed out and distributed among the class as a recommended list.

A 6 Scanning an advertisement/ explaining (sports) rules in writing

Using an advertisement for a sports centre, students practice the skill of scanning a text to find specific information. In role play dialogues they then ask for more detailed information about the activities advertised.
The insight is also gained that when explaining the rules of a sport or game it is practical to follow a certain pattern. As learners put instructions for the game of handball into the correct order they realise, for instance, that it is useful to begin with the equipment needed, the number of players and an explanation of the aim of the game. Using these instructions as a model students then write out the rules for playing one of their favourite sports or games.

1. Finding specific information
The topic can be introduced by a general discussion of sports, for instance which sports are popular with the students, whether they participate in them actively or rather as spectators, whether they would like to do more sports and if so, which ones.
Working in pairs, groups or individually the class then scan the advertisement to locate the information required. They compare results to check that nothing has been left out.

Write down ...

Monday	Tuesday	Wednesday	Thursday	Friday	Saturday	Sunday
aerobics, karate, gymnastics	swimming, aerobics, badminton, judo	swimming, karate, volleyball	swimming, basketball, Chinese kickboxing	swimming, squash, judo	junior football, roller disco, swimming, basketball	swimming, fitness club

2. Asking for and giving information

This task gives more practice in scanning the text and also in asking for and giving information. Pairs of students develop role play dialogues in which one person picks out a section which interests him or her and asks for more details. The 'employee' has to locate the information as quickly as possible. Students take it in turns to make the enquiries. The dialogues can be written down and/or read out to the class. Here are some useful phrases:
– *Good morning. Trafford Sports Centre. Can I help you?*
– *Good morning. This is ... speaking. I wanted to know / I'm interested in ... / Could you please tell me ... / Has the ... course started yet? / How much is the ... class? / I'd like to book for ... / Do I have to book for ...? / Can I hire ...? / How much is it to hire ...? / Is there a ... class? / a class for ...? / How many people are in the ... class? / Where ...? / What should I wear for ...? / What do they do in the fitness club besides ...?*

3. Understanding rules

The activity could take the form of a competition to find out who can do it fastest.

Match two rules ...
tennis: *2, 5*; golf: *3, 8*; basketball: *1, 7*; chess: *4, 6*.

Write down ...
A few minutes are allowed for each student to write down five similar rules to describe either the sports mentioned on the worksheet or different ones. They then take it in turns to ask their partner to guess which activity is being described.

4. Explaining rules

Rules for the game of handball are in the wrong order. Pairs or groups of students correct the order, during which process they become aware of the conventional ordering principles of rules for sports or games, namely that they usually begin with the necessary equipment, number of players and aim of the game.

Can you ...? Decide first ...
Depending on the class students can be given help in deciding on the order. The following headings, for example, could be provided.
– Equipment (Materials) needed/where played
– Number of players/teams
– What is the aim? What does the winner or winning team have to do?
– How long does the game last?
– How does it start?
– What are the rules?

Suggestions for the order will vary, but this is one possibility.

> This team game is similar to football and basketball. It is usually played indoors, on a court with a goal at each end. The ball is round and slightly smaller than a football. There are two teams of 5 or 7 players, a time-keeper and two referees. The aim is to score as many goals as possible.
> A game lasts for an hour and has two 30-minute halves. It begins when one player throws the ball to a member of his or her team from the centre of the court. Except for the goalkeeper players are not allowed to kick the ball. They throw and bounce it towards the goal, stopping and hitting it with any part of the body except the lower legs and feet.

A 6
A 7

> Players can only hold the ball for a maximum of three seconds and cannot take more than three steps while holding it. It can be passed in any direction and also rolled along the ground.
> The only person allowed in the goal area is the goalkeeper.

What is ...?
The rules are for handball.

Think of ...
Using the above model students give a written explanation of the rules of a favourite sport or game without mentioning its name. To check whether the instructions are clear enough they are read out to the class, who should be able to identify the sport. Suggestions can be made for improving the rules.

A 7 Scanning an encyclopedia article / making notes (list)

Students practise the skill of quickly locating specific information in a text by scanning through it, ignoring irrelevant points and focussing on those which interest them. This is followed by a phase of detailed reading. The information is then converted into note form in order to make it easier to learn and remember, a process which involves rearranging the order of the information to correspond to the students' own categories.

1. Before you start reading
Interest in the topic is stimulated by a few questions about Canada. Generally speaking, the reading process is more effective if previous knowledge of the subject is activated first, since the new information can then be more easily incorporated with the old.

Check ...
Groups of learners answer as many questions as possible and mark the ones which are too difficult.

Write down ...
Learners note down anything else they know about the country, also anything they would like to know.

2. Looking for specific information
Students scan the article to find the missing facts. They are instructed to look only for this specific information and to ignore the rest of the text.

Quickly read ...
The answers to the five questions are supplied in the article:
1. Provinces: *Alberta, British Columbia, Manitoba, New Brunswick, Newfoundland, Nova Scotia, Ontario, Prince Edward Island, Quebec, Saskatchewan;* Territories: *the Northwest Territory, Yukon Territory, Nunavut.*
2. *Larger.*
3. *About three quarters of the population live in the strip of land along the US border, mostly in Quebec and Ontario.*
4. *Five.*
5. *Federal constitutional monarchy, member of Commonwealth. Queen Elizabeth as head of state, represented by Governor-General. Prime minister as head of government.*
6. *French.*

Did the article ...?
If the article did not answer the students' own questions about Canada (task 1) they should be encouraged to do some research of their own.

3. Identifying the main points
Students now read the article in detail. After reading it through once to get the general idea they go through it a second time, underlining or highlighting the main points. They compare their results and try to improve them.

Suggestions will vary, but this is one possibility.

> Canada is the world's second largest country after Russia. It stretches over five time zones and is divided into ten provinces (Alberta, British Columbia, Manitoba, New Brunswick, Newfoundland, Nova Scotia, Ontario, Prince Edward Island, Quebec, Saskatchewan) and three territories (the

Northwest Territory, Yukon Territory and Nunavut).
About three quarters of Canada's 30 million people inhabit a relatively narrow strip of land along the US border, concentrated in Quebec and Ontario. The three territories, vast areas of land, are very empty with only 0.3 per cent of the total population. The population as a whole is mostly urban, living in the main cities of Toronto, Montreal, Winnipeg, Calgary, Edmonton, Vancouver and Ottawa, the capital.
For centuries Canada was inhabited by Inuits (Eskimos) and Indians. But from the sixteenth century onwards the British and French began to settle and to fight for power. Today nearly 40 per cent of Canadians have British origins, 27 per cent French, 16 per cent Asian and the remainder are a rich ethnic mix of Germans, Italians, Ukrainians, Dutch, Scandinavians, Poles, Hungarians, Greeks and the native peoples, officially known as the 'First Nations' (3 per cent). During the past thirty years Canada's ethnic mix has changed significantly, mainly because of a more open policy towards immigrants. The government encourages each ethnic group to preserve their own culture.
Canada has two official languages, English and French. Most French-speaking Canadians live in Quebec, where they make up about 78 per cent of the 7 million inhabitants. They feel quite distinct from the rest of the country and are proud of their language and culture, constantly trying to defend it from further anglicization. This has been reflected in a desire for independence from Canada and in growing support for pro-separatist parties.
Canada is a country with enormous natural resources, notably oil, gas, minerals, forests, huge lakes and rivers. It is the world's largest exporter of forest products and a main exporter of fish, furs, wheat and hydroelectricity. It is also an important manufacturing country. Whereas up to the twentieth century the economy was largely based on agriculture, today Canada is one of the most highly industrialized countries in the world.

Politically speaking, Canada is a federal constitutional monarchy and a member of the Commonwealth. The head of state is Britain's Queen Elizabeth II (from 1952 onwards), represented by a Governor-General with formal duties only. The head of government is the prime minister.

4. Putting information into note form
Groups or pairs of learners put the main points into note form and group them together under certain headings. This may entail rearranging the order of the information.

Reduce ...
Depending on the class it may be necessary to provide the categories. Answers will vary. One suggestion:

Size:
– second largest country after Russia
– five time zones

Regions:
– *10 provinces: Alberta, British Columbia, Manitoba, New Brunswick, Newfoundland, Nova Scotia, Ontario, Prince Edward Island, Quebec, Saskatchewan*
– *3 territories: the Northwest Territory, Yukon Territory, Nunavut*

Distribution of population:
– *30 million*
– *three quarters along US border, mainly in Quebec and Ontario, in Toronto, Montreal, Winnipeg, Calgary, Edmonton, Vancouver and Ottawa (capital); mostly urban*
– *Only 0.3 % in territories*

Ethnic composition:
– *from 16th century on, British and French colonised Canada*
– *nearly 40 % have British origins, 27 % French, 16 % Asian, rest Germans, Italians, Ukrainians, Dutch, Scandinavians, Poles, Hungarians, Greeks, 'First Nations' (3 %)*
– *welcome immigration, encourages different cultures*

Quebec:
– 7 million, 78% French-speakers. English and French both official languages.
– proud of language and culture, fight against anglicization, want independence

Economy:
– huge natural resources (oil, gas, minerals, forests, lakes, rivers), largest exporter of forest products, main exporter of fish, furs, wheat, hydroelectricity
– important manufacturing country, one of most highly industrialized countries

Political system:
– federal constitutional monarchy, member of Commonwealth
– head of state Queen Elizabeth II, represented by Governor-General, prime minister as head of government

5. Checking what you have learned
Students check what they have learned by means of a quiz. Pairs of students make up about 8 questions, using the information in the article. They then exchange papers with other pairs and later return them and mark the answers.

A 8 Writing informal letters

Students become familiar with the conventions of informal letters, using the situation of preparing an exchange visit with someone from an English-speaking country.

1. Introducing yourself to a stranger
An informal letter provides a model for the students' own production.

Write back ...
Learners reply to the letter individually, expressing their interest and introducing themselves.

Before you start ...
Students note down some ideas for writing a reply.

Pick out ...
The model letter also provides useful vocabulary for making suggestions and requests:
a) making suggestions:
   – *(Some people in our class) would like to*
   – *wondered if anyone might be interested*
   – *you could*
b) asking for something:
   – *please write back and tell us if*
   – *perhaps you could suggest*

2. Writing an informal letter
With the help of the vocabulary already collected, the tips and the textual model learners write their replies. Sample letters can be read out and possibly improved on.
Students are reminded of the different ways of writing and speaking the date in British and American English.
A model letter is given on the left-hand side of p. 63.

A 9 Writing formal letters: applying for jobs

At some stage most students will probably need to write a formal letter in English, for instance to apply for a job, ask for information, organise a school trip or book a holiday. This unit familiarises them with the conventions of formal letters and in particular of job applications.

1. Jobs
To focus minds on the topic pairs of students talk about any jobs they may already have done. Working in pairs they then ask each other about their further plans after school. They can then relate their findings to the class.

2. Can I help you?
A guessing game revises the word field 'jobs'. The activity can take the form of a competition between groups or teams.

Can you tell ...?
a) Waiter; b) Dentist; c) Postman/postwoman;
d) Someone on the stage, e.g. actor, actress, dancer;

A 8

model letter: formal

Your address

Date

The Manager
South Sands Holiday Camp
Littlehampton BN17 5LF
England

Application for a job as a holiday host

Dear Sir/Madam,

I am writing to apply for a job as a holiday host at your summer camp.

I have had some experience of working with children. Last year I spent two weeks helping to entertain children during their summer holidays. I really enjoyed it and would very much like to do this kind of work again. I am a cheerful, happy sort of person and get on well with children.

I have been learning English for about five years and am quite good at it. Last year I stayed with an English family for three weeks and really enjoyed it. I would love to come to England again this summer.

Unfortunately, I do not play any instruments, but I am quite good at sports and would be able to teach the children how to play volleyball.

Would you please give me some information about working hours and pay. Do you provide accomodation or could you help me to find somewhere to stay?

I enclose a photograph.

Yours sincerely,

(name)

A 9

model letter: informal

Your address

Date

Dear Jenny,

I saw your letter on our school notice-board and was very interested. I've asked some people in our class about it. Some would like to take part in an exchange and others want to think about it first. I would definitely like to come. Even if there are not enough people for a school exchange we could still do it privately, couldn't we?

To introduce myself – I'm nearly sixteen and have been learning English for five years. I enjoy it very much and would love to visit England. I've never been there before. I'd like to stay with a family and go to your school. It sounds great. I like dancing and love going to discos. I also play volleyball. When I have time I like playing computer games.

My parents think an exchange would be a good idea. They would like to have someone from your class to stay with us. My brother Tommy, who is fourteen, would also like it. I'd prefer to exchange with a girl, if possible. She could come to school with me. Our school has a theatre group, too, I also a film club and a choir. The best time would probably be in June or July, before our summer holidays start. We could go and see different places in the afternoons and at weekends. We could also go to the swimming pool.

Please write back soon and tell me if anyone would like to exchange with me or how many of your class want to come. Perhaps you could suggest some dates so we can start thinking about the details. Do you have an e-mail address?

Best wishes,

(name)

e) *Photographer;* f) *Policeman/policewoman;*
g) *Doctor;* h) *Swimming instructor;* k) *Shop assistant*

Can you think ...?
Pairs of learners think up further examples and ask their classmates to guess the answers.

3. Applying for a job
After reading the advertisement students note down the questions which they have about the job and also their qualifications.

First make ...
Answers will vary.
My questions: *working hours, accomodation, pay, free time.* (Students should be reminded not to ask about pay first!)
My qualifications: *fairly good English, cheerful, happy sort of person, enjoy working with children, play (the guitar), sing, play in volleyball team ...*

4. Writing formal letters
The style of formal letters has changed over the past few years. Today the trend is to reduce the number of commas in addresses and dates in order to produce a neater, uncluttered look. Generally, the ending 'Yours sincerely' has replaced the more formal 'Yours faithfully'.
Using the model of a formal letter, the tips, and the vocabulary aids learners write letters applying for the advertised job.
They can then exchange their letters and ask for suggestions for improvements.

Use this model ... (see the right-hand side of p. 63)
For a reminder of how to write the dates see p. 19.

A 10 An informative text/ reorganising information

Students are required to read an informative article about Australia very closely in order to pick out the information needed to label a map of the country. The information is then rearranged in a different order according to specific criteria.

1. Picking out information
The text is read silently. Working individually or in pairs the class then complete the map.

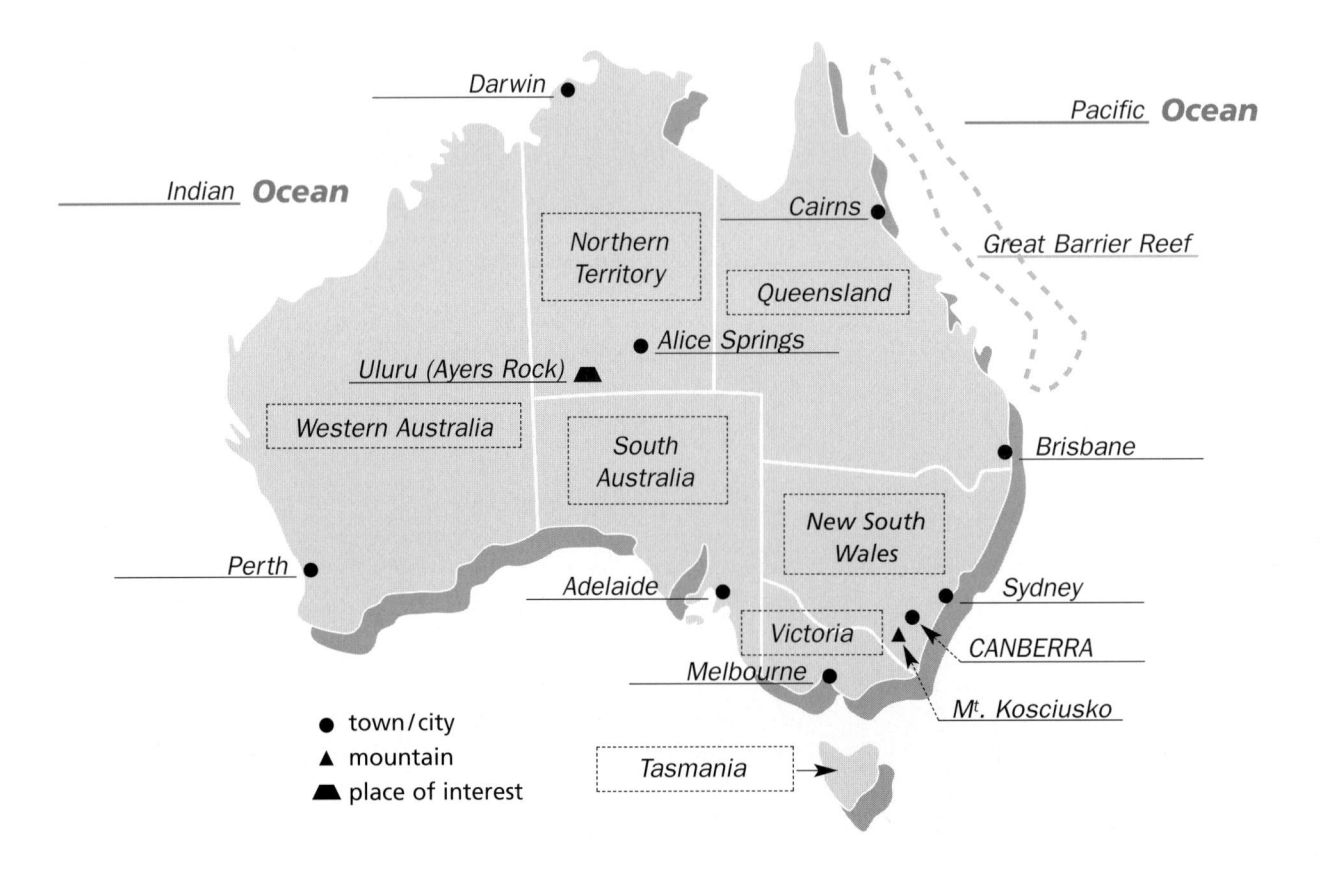

Read …
The map should be labelled as shown on p. 64.

2. Reorganising information
Information about the various states and territories, which is scattered throughout the text, is reorganised according to the given headings and put into note form.

Pick out …

Queensland
– interior dry, used for grazing sheep
– *capital Brisbane*
– *Great Barrier Reef off coast, near Cairns*

New South Wales
– sheep in dry outback
– *capital Sydney (2000 Olympic Games, largest surburban area in the world (nearly 4 million in 1995)*
– *highest mountain Mount Kosciusko (2,228 m)*

South Australia
– *sheep farming in interior*
– *capital Adelaide*

Victoria
– *capital Melbourne*

Northern Territory
– *capital Darwin*
– *Alice Springs, Uluru (Ayers Rock) in outback*

Western Australia
– *capital Perth*
– *minerals, gold, natural gas, diamonds*

3. Check what you have learned
Learners check how much of the information they remember by making up questions about Australia.

Cover …
Students cover up the article and write down five questions about Australia. Pairs of learners take it in turns to ask and answer each other's questions. Only when an attempt has been made to answer all ten questions can the article be consulted.

A 11 Conventional features of instructional texts / writing instructions

Instructions need to be written very clearly so that we can follow them easily. Using information on elementary first aid students become familiar with the conventional features of instructions, regarding both contents and layout.

1. Could you give first aid?
To introduce the topic learners are asked whether they would be able to apply first aid in two particular situations. Suggestions will vary but should include the following information. They can be written in prose or as a list.

1. Someone in your family …
A burn should be cooled immediately with cold water. Keep cooling it for about ten minutes. You should not try to pull any clothes off the burn, but take off anything tight near it, like a watch or ring, because the skin will swell. Then the burn should be covered with a clean, dry cloth, made of material which will not stick to the skin, such as a handkerchief. You should not put any kind of cream on the burn.

Alternatively: *Burns*
a) *Cool the skin immediately with cold water/by gently pouring cold water over it. Keep cooling for about ten minutes. Don't pull any clothes off.*
b) *Remove anything tight near the burn (watch, rings), before the injury starts to swell.*
c) *Cover the burn with a clean, dry piece of cloth, made of material which will not stick to the skin, such as a handkerchief.*
d) *Don't put on any kind of cream.*

2. You are playing volleyball …
Straighten the person's knee and pull the foot up towards the shin as far as it will go.

2. Changing prose into a set of instructions
A set of instructions written in prose is put into a more suitable form.

What do you think …?
Learners should recognise that the instructions are too long. In an emergency no one would have time to read them.

A11 Teaching notes

A11

Rewrite them …

Learners work individually or in pairs and then exchange their results with others, who make comments and offer suggestions for improvements. Suggestions will vary, but they should contain the following information:

> In an accident it is important to act quickly:
> 1. Give first aid <u>immediately</u> to stop the injury from getting worse.
> 2. <u>Get help</u> as quickly as possible.
> 3. Make the patient comfortable <u>without moving</u> them too much.
>   WARNING: If you think something might be broken <u>don't move</u> them.

3. Characteristic features of instructions

A comparison between the instructions in task 2 and the students' work illustrates the conventional features of instructions, which help to make them clearer and easier to read.

Compare …

Although the students' work will vary slightly, they will probably all have used the following features:
Type of sentences: *Short, very easy to understand.*
Verb forms: *Imperative (Give, Get, Make, Don't).*
Effect: *directly addresses reader, making them feel more involved.*
Layout:
– *Numbering makes it easier to see each point;*
– *Underlinings and capital letters make certain words stand out, you notice them immediately and will remember them better.*

Look at …

Using their knowledge of the characteristic features of instructive texts students are now able to recognise the faults in a badly written set of instructions. They should also realise that certain vital information is missing.

Would they help …?

The instructions are not very helpful because they are not clear enough. The sentences are too long and complex. There would not be time to read them in an emergency. No explanation is given as to why the legs should be raised. An illustration would be helpful.

Is there anything else …?

We are not told how to recognise when people are going to faint. What do they look like?

Students are asked to produce an improved version of this set of instructions in the following task (part of the poster).

4. Writing a set of instructions

Using their knowledge of the conventions of instructive texts pairs or groups of students put lengthy prose instructions into a form in which they would be more helpful in an emergency.

Rewrite …

Suggestions will vary, but the poster could look something like this.

> FIRST AID
>
> <u>Treating simple injuries</u>
> If someone has had an accident
> 1. FIND OUT exactly what is wrong.
> 2. DON'T panic. This will help the injured person to relax.
> 3. Ask if the person feels there is ANYTHING WRONG, e.g. that they cannot move an arm or a leg.
> 4. Look for CLUES: Is the skin cold and sweaty, hot and dry? Is the face very pale or red? Can you see any blood?
>
> <u>Fainting</u>
> 1. Recognise the SIGNS: pale face, sweaty skin, weakness, sometimes feeling of sickness.
> 2. LAY the person DOWN and RAISE their legs a little so the blood flows towards the brain. *(An illustration would be useful here. Students could draw simple stick figures.)*
> 3. Make sure there is plenty of FRESH AIR.
> 4. When the patient starts feeling better help them to sit up, SLOWLY.
>
> <u>Nose bleeds</u>
> 1. Sit down and BEND SLIGHTLY over a sink or bowl to catch the blood.
> 2. Breathe through your mouth. HOLD YOUR

> NOSE between fingers and thumb at the top end of the nose. You might have to press for up to ten minutes. *(Students should illustrate this point.)*
> 3. UNDO any tight clothing round the neck.
> 4. Soak a piece of cloth in COLD WATER and put it over the top of the nose.
>   – DON'T TILT your head BACK *(illustration, with a line through it or crossed out)* because the blood will run down your throat and make you choke.
>   – DON'T PUSH anything up your nose, like cotton wool.
>   – DON'T BLOW your nose for a few hours when the bleeding has stopped.
>
> Bruises
> 1. Put some ice (or a bag of frozen peas) in a plastic bag.
> 2. Leave the ice-bag on the bruise for about half an hour.

A12 Identifying the main ideas in a newspaper article / linking ideas

Learners are given practice in identifying the main ideas in a text. They are also made aware of the various functions of different link-words and phrases, for example to announce a consequence *(therefore)* or to signal that what follows is contrasted with previous ideas *(whereas)*.

1. Talking about spending money
The topic 'spending money' (or 'pocket money') is introduced by a brief discussion of the students' own spending habits. They then fill in the table.

Do you ever …?
Besides introducing the topic the table also provides the opportunity to clarify some of the terms which appear in the article, such as the categories 'leisure goods' and 'leisure services'. The table is filled in using rough percentages rather than figures in order to avoid embarrassing comparisons.

What do you spend …? Is there …?
The class briefly discuss whether there are any major differences in the spending habits of the boys and girls.

2. A comparison with British teenagers
The article is read twice, firstly for gist, then in detail. The second time students are asked to identify the main ideas by
– underlining them and reducing them further to key words or phrases
– thinking of subheadings for each paragraph.

… underline … Reduce …
After underlining the most important passages students try to reduce them further to key words and phrases (indicated in the following by underlining). Results will differ slightly, but the following main ideas should be identified.

> British teenagers have on average £8.30 a week spending money. Most of it … goes on food … Next come leisure goods … The third most popular item is clothing.
> Whilst boys and girls spend roughly the same amount of money, they tend to use it differently …
> Most of the young people interviewed recognised the importance of managing their money properly … they were all very much aware of the influence of advertising …
> Where parents were the main source of income there was sometimes resentment if they wanted to know how the money was spent. Yet some youngsters welcomed their parents' involvement …
> Whereas some teenagers manage on the pocket money they get from their parents, others prefer to earn their own … money means much more to young people than simply buying things …
> Many teenagers find it unfair to expect their parents to pay for everything.

A12 Teaching notes

A13

Give …
Suggestions will vary.
1. How British teenagers spend their money
2. Boys and girls spend their money differently
3. Managing pocket money
4. Pocket/Spending money from parents
5. Earning your own money
6. Responsibility towards parents

3. Recognising more and less important ideas
In order to identify the main ideas in a text it is also essential to be able to recognise the less important ones. Clues can be picked up from the words and phrases used to link the ideas. Expressions like 'for instance' and 'for example' signal that the following material illustrates something which has already been said; 'but' shows that what follows will be contrasted with a previous idea.

Look at …
The words 'for instance' show that this sentence is an example of something which has already been said.
(Similarly, the quotations throughout the passage are also illustrations of points already made, e.g. "If I go shopping …" [paragraph 4]; One girl pointed out, "Money …" [paragraph 5]).

Find …
'Indeed, they seem very skilled …' (paragraph 3) has the function of emphasising or reinforcing something which has already been said. (Most of the young people … managing their money properly).

Look for more …
Working in pairs or groups learners match the link-words in the article with their function. Numbers refer to paragraphs.
A. To contrast ideas or to contradict what has been said before: *whilst (2), although (2), yet (4), whereas (5), however (6);*
B. To list a number of ideas: *most of it … next … the third … (1); another (finding) (3);*
C. To explain a consequence: *and so (6);*
D. To introduce examples or illustrations: *for instance (3); for example (5);*
E. To underline or rephrase what has already been said: *indeed (3).*

Can you add …?
More examples are found for each category, e.g.:
A. To contrast ideas or to contradict what has been said before: *but, though, nevertheless, in spite of, despite, on the one hand … on the other*
B. To list a number of ideas: *first(ly), second(ly), then, in addition, one point is that … another point … a last point, finally*
C. To explain a consequence: *consequently, therefore, as a result, thus*
D. To introduce examples or illustrations: *such as, like*
E. To underline or rephrase what has already been said: *in other words, that is to say, similarly.*

4. Your opinion
Ideas in the article provide stimuli for the class to write a short text expressing their own views on pocket money. They can also draw on their own experience to suggest ways of augmenting their spending money, for instance by part-time jobs. Their knowledge of link words should be used to connect the ideas in a logical, fluent way.

Further work
The class can be encouraged to keep track of their spending habits over the next few days (e.g. *Make a list of how you spend your next lot of pocket money. Is there any way you could save more?*). At a later date they could discuss the outcome of this project.

A13 Argumentative text/writing a balanced argument

An article discussing the advantages and disadvantages of school uniform provides a model for the effective presentation of arguments. Using these guidelines students produce a similar text of their own, arguing the points for and against the proposal in a balanced way.

1. Thinking about different points of view
The topic is introduced by a brief discussion of school uniform. Pairs or groups of students collect a few arguments and note them down in the table. By a show of hands the class then indicate

how much support there is for each side. After reading the arguments in the worksheet text a second vote will ascertain whether there has been any significant change of opinion.

Think of ...
Working in pairs or groups the class collect arguments for and against school uniform.

Read ...
Students read the text silently, then add any new arguments to their tables, using either their own words or those from the text. The following points are raised in the article: (see table below).

Have any of you ...
A second vote ascertains whether anyone has changed their mind after the discussion. If so, they should give their reasons. The class could be encouraged to do a survey in their own school to find out how their fellow students feel about school uniform.

Suggest ...
In groups students make suggestions for reducing conflicts caused by jealousy over fashionable clothes, for instance through discussions, by having one day a week when everyone comes in their oldest clothes, or by projects to raise understanding for those with less money to spend.

Further task
The class can be asked to think up some ideas for a summer and a winter school uniform, expressing them either verbally or as a sketch.

2. Presenting both sides of the argument
The article is analysed to illustrate the conventional structure of argumentative texts. Attention is particularly drawn to the various linking words, which have the function of connecting ideas in a way which makes for a fluent text (c.f. A 12,3).

Examine how ... Collect ...
The article is combed for useful words and phrases for writing argumentative texts and put into the given categories. Some phrases can be used in the two sections in which arguments are listed, e.g. *many (young) people feel, they also say.* Students then add more suggestions of their own.

1. Introduction:
   Lately there has been a lot of debate about (whether)
   Further suggestions:
   People have been wondering/discussing; suggestions have been made for

2. Arguments for school uniform:
   Those who support the idea believe; another advantage/a further argument in favour of; many (young) people feel; they also say; another argument (which is sometimes heard)
   Further suggestions:
   Some people argue that; they also believe; it has been suggested that; for several reasons; one reason/point/argument is ..., another ...; first(ly), ... second(ly); then; in addition; a last point; finally

3. Arguments against school uniform:
   However, many (young) people feel; others point out; they also say; another argument (which is sometimes heard)
   In this section it is useful to collect words for contrasting ideas, e.g.:
   although; however; other people disagree; they argue that; whereas; whilst; yet;

Arguments for school uniform	Arguments against school uniform
– fewer clothes are stolen, not so much worrying about clothes – less pressure on parents, less embarrassment – better behaviour out of school – more pressure to attend school – creates common identity, solidarity	– boring to wear same clothes all the time – can't express personality through clothes – colour, style might not suit everyone – young people have to learn to live with social inequality

A 13 Teaching notes

A 14

nevertheless; in spite of; despite; on the one hand … on the other; in contrast (to); one advantage … the disadvantage

4. <u>Conclusion/writer's opinion:</u>
we have come to the conclusion that; there are more arguments in favour of; after all
Further suggestions:
Although some people might argue that; I think; my own feelings/opinion; therefore; after looking at/considering both sides of the question I have come to the conclusion that; one reason is; and so I think; to sum up / I'd like to sum up the main points; I think I have shown

3. Writing a balanced argument
Students write their own argumentative article, using the guidelines on the worksheet. The instruction not to refer back to the original text encourages them to use their own words. The article should present a balanced point of view.

A 14 Oral presentation of written texts / making notes, summarising

Students are frequently required to give oral presentations of the contents of written texts. In this unit they learn to become good presenters, which entails converting written texts into spoken language and the interpersonal skills of maintaining eye contact, checking to see if the audience is following and taking charge of a discussion.

The topic selected is the modern mixture of English and German commonly known as 'Denglish'. As students learn the various techniques of oral presentation, they also become aware of the problems connected with the growing influence of English on the German language.

1. For and against 'Denglish'
The topic, 'Denglish', can be introduced by asking the class to write down English words or phrases which are often used in Germany in the fields of fashion, music, television or sports. A time limit of 3 or 4 minutes should be set.
Some suggestions:

<u>Fashion</u>: *Collection, Design/Designer, Fashion, Leggings, Lifestyle, Outfit, Relax-Look, Slip, Sweatshirt.*
<u>Music</u>: *Band, CD-Player, Charts, Deejay, Event, Festival, Hit, Open Air, Song, Sound, Studio.*
<u>Television</u>: *Cartoon, Comedy, Entertainer, Nonsense, (Talk) Show, Star, Thriller, TV.*
<u>Sports</u>: *Fitness-Center, Inline skates, Jogging, Kickboard, Mountain Bike, Pace, Skateboard, Snowboard, Speed, Team.*

In order to sensitise students to the problems attached to Denglish and to prepare them for the article they are then asked to briefly consider whether the increasing influence of English on German is a good thing or not. A few opinions can be collected and noted down on the board or OHP. At this stage there should not be a long discussion. After the oral presentation of the arguments in the article the class will have plenty of opportunity to air their views.

Read this article …
Silently, learners read the article and mark the most important points. They may need to read it through once for gist, then again for detail. Unknown words should be guessed at as far as possible. Where they are not absolutely essential for understanding they can be ignored.
Comparing their results helps students to decide on the main points. There will be variations, but this is one possibility (c. f. p. 71).

Further task
Students can be asked to find:
1. the original BE or AE meanings of the 'Denglish' words:
   – Evergreen – *a bush which has green leaves all year round*
   – Flipper – *1. a flat part of the body of some sea animals, like seals, used for swimming; 2. a long, flat piece of rubber worn on the feet when swimming*
   – Oldtimer – *an old man*
2. the BE or AE equivalents of the 'Denglish' words:
   Evergreen – *golden oldie*; Flipper – *pinball machine*; Oldtimer – *vintage car*; Dressman – *male model*; Talkmaster – *chat show host*; Wellness – *well-being, health*

Since the beginning of the 1990s more and more English words and expressions have come into the German language, making it quite difficult to understand at times. Older people often cannot interpret what their children or grandchildren say. This is not a new development, every generation creates its own jargon, but there has been nothing quite like this latest phenomenon. English, or rather a jumbled mixture of English and German known as 'Denglish', is rapidly dominating every walk of life – fashion, music, the media, sports, business, technology, advertising. One striking example is Lufthansa's advertisement 'Mit dem neuen Standby oneway Upgrade-Voucher kann direkt beim Check-in das Ticket aufgewertet werden' which hardly includes any German at all.

Although some people are horrified at the increasing influence of English on German, others argue that since language is a living thing change is a natural state. All languages borrow from each other and German is no exception. Whereas it previously borrowed from Latin, Greek and French, now it is from English.

Often this is unavoidable, for example when new developments are taken over from a different culture and there are no words to describe them in the native language. At other times it is more practical to use the foreign word. Imagine, for instance, having to describe *spaghetti*. It is far easier to simply use the original than to order 'those long, thin noodles'. Some imported words have become so integrated that they are no longer regarded as foreign.

Many English words are preferred because of their brevity and succinctness, such as *stress* (shorter than 'Anstrengung'), *fast-food* or *workaholic*. However, today it appears that English expressions are not being borrowed for such practical reasons, but to demonstrate modernity or *coolness*. Why else should a local phone call be a *CityCall* and what is the advantage of calling a baker's a *Backshop*? The danger is not so much the flood of English words in itself, but rather the frequent mistakes, such as *last not least* instead of 'last but not least' or the introduction of the apostrophe *'s* into German, resulting in wrong usage such as '*Rudis'* Fundstube' or '*Info's* hier'. Some English words have been given different meanings to their original ones, for instance the *Handy*. In English this is not a noun, but an adjective, meaning 'useful'. The translation of the German 'Handy' is 'mobile phone'. Other examples are *Evergreen*, *Flipper* and *Oldtimer*. Some so-called 'English' words have simply been invented, although they do not actually exist in English. An English speaker, for instance, would not understand the word 'Backshop' and might think it was a shop around the back of a building, like 'back door', or even a shop where you can take things back if you do not like them. Other examples are *Dressman*, *Talkmaster*, or *Wellness*. In other cases English and German have been combined to create new words, such as *anturnen*, *chatten*, *checken*, *relaxen*.

It can be argued that German is enriched by words from other languages and that 'Denglish' expresses the flexibility and openness of the German language and people. On the other hand, when words are wrongly used they do not contribute to international communication, as illustrated by the term 'Handy', which native speakers of English would not understand. Eventually Denglish results in a kind of pidgin English. And as to openness, other countries, including Britain and America, do not regard Germany as more modern or open because of their jumbled mixture of German and English. On the contrary, they find it rather ridiculous.

Many Germans oppose what they see as the public undermining of the German language, complaining that words like *clever*, *Event*, *happy*, *last minute*, *Highlight*, *Make-up*, *Power*, *relax*, *Sale*, *Shopping* and *Slow motion* have completely replaced their German equivalents. It has even been suggested that fines be imposed, for instance on taxi drivers displaying the English notice "Fasten your seat belt" instead of "Bitte anschnallen".

A 14 Teaching notes

Additional information

The German Language Union has compiled the following lists of 'Denglish' expressions which they find
a) annoying because the German equivalents are equally expressive: aftershave, agreement, aircondition (the correct BE/AE version is airconditioning), airline, airmail, art director etc.
b) borderline cases: action, airbag, apartment, approach, baby (child), bar, band, bestseller etc.
c) English words which are being taken over because they are shorter and more succinct than the German equivalents: clinch, clown, countdown, doping, flirt, freak, gentleman etc.
d) 'Pseudo-English', i.e. words with different meanings in German to their original English ones or which have been invented by Germans: Callboy, Dressman, Service Point, Showmaster, Smoking, Spot (only exist in German, English equivalents 'male prostitute, male model, information desk, show host, tuxedo, commercial');
e) Computer language: Backup, Blank, booten, Compiler, Computer, deleten etc.
f) Sports and leisure activities: Champion, Champions League, Championship, Crosscountry, Drummer, Finish, Freeclimbing etc.

For more information see the Internet page www.vds-ev.de/denglisch/anglizismen/anglizismen_a.htm

Just for fun

The following Denglish poem was published on the Internet by Klaus Christen, 10. Januar 2001, www.f23.parsimony.net/forum51035/messages/141.htm.

Weihnachten ist over and trotzdem overall zu all times!

When the last Kalender-sheets
flattern through the winter-streets
and Dezemberwind is blowing,
then ist everybody knowing
that it is not allzuweit:
she does come – the Weihnachtszeit.

All the Menschen, Leute, people
flippen out of ihr warm Stueble,
run to Kaufhof, Aldi, Mess,
make Konsum and business.
Kaufen this and jene Dings
and the Churchturmglocke rings.

Manche holen sich a Taennchen,
when this brennt, they cry "Attention",
Rufen for the Feuerwehr:
"Please come quick to loeschen her!"
Goes the Taennchen of in Rauch,
they are standing on the Schlauch.

In the kitchen of the house
mother makes the Christmasschmaus.
She is working, schufting, bakes,
Hit is now her Yoghurtkeks.
And the Opa says als Tester:
"We are killed bis to Silvester."
Then he fills the last Glas wine –
yes, this is the Christmastime!

etc.

2. Preparing a talk
In preparation for giving a short talk on Denglish to the whole class, pairs or groups of students make notes, following the instructions on the worksheet. At this stage no additional arguments should be included.

3. Giving the talk
It is important to realise that giving a talk is a two-way process. The speaker is not on trial, but has the role of a leader, responsible for helping the audience to concentrate and to follow what is being said.

Imagine your friend …
Pairs or groups of learners collect ideas for helping the speaker to get over any nervousness before and while giving a talk.
Ideas will vary. Some suggestions:

Before you start breathe deeply.
Try to relax.
Do not start until the room is quiet. Look confidently round the room and smile.
Keep your head up while you are speaking.

List ...
Students suggest some ways in which a speaker can keep an audience interested. It is important to help listeners to follow the talk and also to make them feel involved.
Some suggestions:

> **Helping listeners to follow the talk**
> – Speak *slowly and clearly.*
> – Check *if everyone can hear you.*
> – Use *short sentences which are easy to follow. Talk to your audience naturally.*
> – Do not *simply read your notes out, only use them as a reminder.*
> – Vary *the speed and tone of your voice. Do not talk too fast.*
> – Write *important points down (board, OHP, handout). Sum up frequently. Emphasize important ideas and repeat them.*
> – Make *your talk more interesting by using different materials, e.g. visual examples.*
> – Check *your watch. If you run out of time leave things out as you go along.*
> – *Slow down at the end to add impact.*
>
> **Making the audience feel involved**
> – Keep *looking at all your listeners.*
> – Check *that people can follow you.*
> – Encourage *them to stop you if they cannot follow.*
> – Use *rhetorical questions.*

4. The audience's role
Before addressing a larger audience learners practise by addressing either a small group or a partner. During this talk the listener(s) answer the questions on the worksheet and later make suggestions for improvements. Students take it in turns to be speakers and listeners. If they work in groups there will probably be some who will not have the chance to speak, but they are still gaining valuable experience. Later some of the talks can be addressed to the whole class.

A15 Debating / writing a poem

In this unit students learn debating skills, comprising the ability to present ideas in a convincing way, to listen to and react appropriately to others and to develop discussions constructively. They are also encouraged to develop their skills in creative writing by composing a poem connected with the topic 'homework'.

1. A survey
The subject of the debate, 'homework', is introduced by a survey in which pairs of learners interview each other and then report their findings to the class.

2. Preparing for a debate
In preparation for a debate on 'homework' groups of students think about their own experiences with it and collect arguments for and against homework. It should be clear that at this stage the aim is to learn how to present an argument, not to express personal views. Consequently, individuals may have to present opinions which they themselves do not support.

First think about ...
Learners reflect about the different aims which homework can have and about the kinds of tasks which they find the most helpful or the most distasteful.

Split the class ...
Some suggestions: see table on page 74.

Take a vote ...
A vote is taken before and after the debate in order to ascertain whether or not the students' opinions are altered by the discussion.

3. Debating behaviour
Students become familiarised with the technique of debating. The first step is to establish rules of conduct.

... set out ...
With the help of the vocabulary aids the class set out rules for the debate.
Some suggestions:

A15 Teaching notes

Arguments supporting homework	Arguments against homework
– not enough time to cover all the work during lessons – some tasks take a long time (understanding English texts, learning vocabulary), so best to do them at home – at home students can work at their own pace – often easier to concentrate at home because quieter – learn to work on your own, organise your time – parents can see what children are doing at home	– students need to relax when they get home – not enough time for other interests – pressurises parents, sometimes whole family, because can't always plan to do things together; sometimes causes stress within family – unfair to those with nowhere to work at home – if you do not understand the homework you cannot always get help at home

– *You should(n't)/Don't interrupt, be rude, get emotional, attack people personally, lose your temper*
– *Listen to what others say/Let other people talk, finish what they are saying*
– *Be polite, stay calm*
– *If you disagree with someone give your reasons*

4. The debate
Students learn that speakers are appointed on the strength of their ability to present arguments convincingly, regardless of their own personal convictions on the issue in question.

Choose ...
Four speakers are chosen to represent four different positions: arguments for and against homework from the point of view of adults and students. They take up their position in front of the class and decide which of each pair should speak first.

The speakers' presentations are followed by a general discussion and a second vote. If anyone has changed their mind they could give their reasons.

5. A poem about homework
Working in groups, the class tries to continue with the poem, making use of the vocabulary provided or using their own words. The results are then read out.

Can you go on?
The original poem, by Trevor Millum is as follows:

The song of the homeworkers

Homework moanwork
Cross it out and groanwork
Homework neatwork
Keeps you off the streetwork
Homework moanwork
Cross it out and groanwork
Homework roughwork
When *you've had enoughwork*
Homework moanwork
Cross it out and groanwork
Homework dronework
Do it on your ownwork
Homework moanwork
Cross it out and groanwork
Homework gloomwork
Gaze around the roomwork
Homework moanwork
Cross it out and groanwork
Homework guesswork
Book is in a messwork
Homework moanwork
Cross it out and groanwork
Homework rushwork
Do it on the buswork
Homework moanwork
Cross it out and groanwork
Homework hatework
Hand your book in latework
Homework moanwork
Cross it out and groan groan

GROANWORK.

A 16 Understanding an explanatory text/ summarising non-fiction

An article explaining how the memory and brain work provides the opportunity to practise the skills of making notes and writing summaries. When summarising any text it is always important to use clear language and to link the ideas logically, but this is especially the case with summaries of explanatory texts. Expressions which help the reader to follow explanations are, for example, *this is shown/illustrated by the fact that ...; this does not mean that ...*

1. Test your memory
The topic is introduced by a questionnaire to test the students' own memories. They should realise that memory can be improved by training and are encouraged to visit a library to find more information. After completing the questionnaire the class can briefly compare their results.

2. Find out more about your memory
Learners check their understanding of the article in a question and answer dialogue.

Read ... carefully ...
The warning that students will later be asked to discuss the article from memory should ensure that an effort is made to understand and remember the contents. It is read individually, in silence. Any unknown words should be guessed at.

Write down ...
Each student writes down five questions about the memory and brain which are raised in the article. Working in pairs they take it in turns to ask each question and the respective partner tries to answer it in his or her own words, from memory. If learners have difficulty formulating questions the following vocabulary can be provided: *What is (the cause of) ...? Is memory (connected with) ...? How can/are ...? What happens when ...? How can we improve ...?*

Questions will differ, but here are some possibilities:
- *What happens when the brain records a new impression? (It is transferred firstly into the 'short-term memory' then into the 'long-term' one).*
- *Which is more likely to be damaged by an accident, illness or drugs? (The short-term memory).*
- *What is usually the cause of a bad memory? (Problems in recalling things).*
- *What theories are there about why we forget things? (Memories gradually fade or become distorted; the new things we learn interfere with or replace the old ones; we may want to forget certain things).*
- *How does the brain cope with the additional material which is put into it? (It builds more pathways).*
- *Is there anything you can do about a bad memory? (Yes, train it, for example by using mnemonics.).*

3. Making notes
In preparation for writing a summary of the article the main ideas are noted down in a mind map. The maps can be compared and improved on.

4. Writing summaries
When summarising – or writing – explanatory texts it is especially important to use expressions which make for clarity and help readers to follow the explanation. Before writing their own summaries the class comb the article for such useful phrases.

Pick out ...
The following words and phrases from the text are useful for linking ideas and for giving explanations:
- <u>linking</u>: *whereas, by contrast, however, whilst, instead, although, for example/instance*
- <u>explanations</u>: *when (the brain/we ...) it ...; this is shown by the fact that ...; there are four ...; one is that ...; another ...; a third possibility ...; finally, ...; (learning new things) does not mean that ...; this is illustrated by the fact that ... .*

Additional words and phrases can be provided:
- <u>linking</u>: *nevertheless, yet, therefore, so, since, as, such as, like, thus, consequently, as a result, on the contrary, instead, in spite of, despite.*

A 16 Teaching notes
A 17

– *explanations:* this means that …; this explains/is why …; the important thing is …; the problem with this is …; the implication is that …; if … then; as a result; another way …; there are (three) main points; firstly …; secondly …; another key point is …

The length of the summary should be limited, either by number of words or in terms of time.

A 17 Understanding a literary text/ summarising fiction

This unit familiarises students with some techniques for summarising the contents of literary texts. Although a certain amount of interpretation is involved, summaries of the contents are not full-blown 'literary interpretations'.

The specific skills entailed in summarising fiction become clear in contrast to summaries of non-fictional material such as the informative article in A 16. Whereas the referents of non-literary texts are identifiable with the real world, those of literary works are not. The characters, places, times and events stem from the writer's imagination and create their own frame of reference. Consequently, everything which is not directly expressed or which does not become clear through the literary context is left to the reader's imagination. Thus the question, taken from a literary text, 'A man? How could a man be a teacher?' cannot be understood without the context. It could be interpreted in various ways – He/She (we do not know who the speaker is) was surprised/horrified that a man and not a woman was a teacher/wondered why a man should have chosen to be a teacher, of all things/ could not understand that they had selected a man for the post etc. In fact, the sentence is taken from the extract which is to be studied in this unit, the science fiction story *The Fun They Had* by Isaac Asimov (l. 54).

Summarising literary texts, then, involves more explanation than is the case with non-fiction. Besides the necessity of clarifying the referents (characters, places, times and events), students also realise that the feelings and attitudes of the characters have to be verbalised. The question in the above example 'A man? How could a man be a teacher?' might have been an expression of surprise, anger, delight or horror. In a summary the characters' feelings need to be made explicit, for example '… was amazed that a man should be clever enough to be a teacher'.

1. Science fiction
The extract can be introduced by a brief discussion of the appeal of science fiction. Students mention any sci-fi books and films they have read or seen and explain why they liked or disliked them. Part of the genre's fascination derives from the futuristic environments and the fact that the events described are often feasible because they develop from trends which are already visible.

Read …
Students read the story to themselves, guessing the meaning of any unknown words. Depending on the class it may be necessary to read it more than once.

2. Starting a summary
As students summarise the first few lines of the extract they will notice the necessity of explaining the context, especially if their imagined reader does not know the text at all. Besides giving details about the setting and characters, it is also necessary to verbalise the characters' reactions, e.g. 'Margie and Tommy were amazed/it was a wonderful discovery'.

Write a summary …
Students are allowed a few minutes to summarise the first few lines of the extract. Working in pairs they then read the results out to each other and make suggestions for improvements. It may be helpful to provide vocabulary aids, such as *The incident, the setting/to set a story.*

Answer will vary. One possibility:
The incident is set in the year 2155. A girl, Margie, writes in her diary that she and a boy called Tommy have found a book. To them this was an amazing discovery/something really strange/wonderful. From her grandfather Margie knows that many years ago stories were always printed on paper.

3. Summarising conversations

When summarising conversations not only the contents need reporting, the speakers' emotions and attitudes also have to be verbalised.

Summarise ...
By reading their summaries out to each other students become aware of the changes which need making, for instance the necessity of verbalising the characters' reactions. The following vocabulary aids can be provided: *to be surprised/amazed, cannot understand, to wonder, to suppose, to think, to ask, to explain/tell.*

One suggestion:
Margie and Tommy are surprised/amazed to find that/cannot understand why the words in the book do not move or even disappear, like they do on a screen. Tommy wonders what happened to books when people had read them. He supposes they just threw them away. He thinks it is better to use television screens because it is not such a waste. When Margie asks him where he found the book he explains that it was in the attic. He tells her it is about school.

4. Writing a correct summary

Learners are given a summary of lines 22–67, in which some details are wrong. They correct the mistakes and at the same time acquire vocabulary and structures which are useful for summarising literary texts in general and the next section of Asimov's story in particular:
– *verbalising feelings: (Margie) cannot understand how/why/what ..., hates, is hurt because, thinks, wonders why, laughs at her because, does not believe (him when he says) ...*
– *reporting direct speech: (Tommy) explains, tells her ...*

Read this summary ...
Working in pairs or groups students identify and correct the mistakes.

One correct version could be as follows:
Margie cannot understand how anyone could write about school. She hates school, especially geography. Recently an inspector came and slowed her mechanical geography teacher down.

Tommy explains to her that the school described in the book is the kind which existed centuries ago. Margie is hurt because she does not know as much about it as Tommy. She cannot understand that the school had a man as a teacher, not a machine. She thinks men are not clever enough. Tommy laughs at her because she does not know anything about the old type of school, for instance that there was a special building for it. Margie is surprised when he tells her that children of the same age used to learn the same things.

Working in pairs ...
Pairs or groups of students give an oral chain summary of the rest of the extract, formulating one sentence each. The results are written down and reduced until they only comprise the most important points. They can then be compared with the work of other groups or pairs.

One suggestion:
Margie is surprised to hear that all the children used to be taught in the same way. She wants to know more about the old schools.
However, before they have finished reading Margie has to go inside for school. In her schoolroom, next to her bedroom, her mechanical teacher is already switched on. She has school at the same time every weekday. Reluctantly, she starts her maths lesson, but is thinking what fun it must have been in the old days when all the children learned together in one room and when they had people as teachers instead of machines.

5. Thinking about the story

Orally or in writing the class discuss the implications of the story.

Further task
Learners can summarise a short story or a novel which they have enjoyed reading. They should be given an idea of the approximate length. All the summaries can then be put up on a notice board as recommendations for others.

A 18 Teaching notes

A 18 Understanding descriptive techniques/ describing physical appearance

Students become aware of the ways in which fictional characters are presented, in this case through descriptions of their physical appearance. The unit progresses from a description focussing more on physical features (task 2), to one in which the link between appearance and personality is explicit and to a third where this link is implicit, requiring the readers to draw their own conclusions (task 3).
Using the literary extracts as models learners write similar descriptions of their own.

1. Describing people's appearance
A brainstorming session reactivates vocabulary to describe physical appearances. The activity can take the form of a competition between pairs, groups or two halves of the class.

List ... The vocabulary can be collected on the board or OHP.

Think of ... Again, the activity can take the form of a competition.

2. Contrasting appearances
The extract focusses mainly on the physical appearance of the two men rather than on their personalities.

Read this description ...
Students first read the extract through silently, then again to pick out the relevant words which describe the men's size, the general appearance of their body, their movements, features, hands and arms. (See table below.)

How does ...?
The author makes the description of the second man's way of walking particularly vivid by comparing it with the slow, heavy movements of a bear.

Explain ...
The contrast makes the whole description more dramatic. It also arouses the reader's interest. We wonder what their relationship is like, if they are so different. Do they quarrel? How did they get together?

3. Appearance and personality
The extract from R. Dahl goes further than the previous one by not only describing a character's physical appearance, but by also making an explicit link between appearance and personality.

Underline ...

> If a person has ugly thoughts, it begins to show on the face. And when that person has ugly thoughts every day, every week, every year, the face gets uglier and uglier until it gets so ugly you can hardly bear to look at it.
> A person who has good thoughts cannot ever be ugly. You can have a wonky nose and a crooked mouth and a double chin and stick-out teeth, but if you have good thoughts they will shine out of your face like sunbeams and you will always look lovely.
> Nothing shone out of Mrs Twit's face.
> In her right hand she carried a walking-stick. She used to tell people this was because she had warts growing on the sole of her left foot and walking was painful. But the real reason she carried a stick was so that she could hit things with it, things like dogs and cats and small children.

	First man	Man behind
size, general appearance of body	small, every part of him was defined	huge, wide, sloping shoulders
movements	quick	walked heavily, dragging his feet
features	dark face, restless eyes, sharp, strong features, thin, bony nose	shapeless face, large, pale eyes
hands and arms	small strong hands, slender arms	heavy hands, arms did not move much, but hung loosely

In the extract from Chandler readers are required to use their powers of deduction to recognise the link between appearance and personality. The terms 'explicit' and 'implicit' are introduced to explain the difference in Dahl's and Chandler's techniques.

As you read …
Students can work either in pairs or individually, comparing their answers.
The man seems to be very concerned with his appearance. He dresses fashionably and his hair is carefully arranged. His white suit suggests that he does not do the kind of work where he might get dirty. In fact, the conclusion could be drawn that he might not do any work at all.

Can you explain …?
In the extract from 'The Twits' the link between appearance and personality is explicit, which means that it is pointed out to the readers ('Why would that happen? I'll tell you why'). Chandler, on the other hand, lets the readers draw their own conclusions. The connection between appearance and personality is implicit.

4. Writing your own descriptions
Using the extracts as models and with the help of the tips the class write their own descriptions of a real, fictional or imaginary character. They restrict themselves to descriptions of physical appearance, but can choose in how far appearance should be linked with personality.
Students can read their descriptions out to each other and make suggestions for improvements before reading them out to the class.

A19 Direct and indirect characterisation/ continuing a story

Students learn that the authors of fictional works employ narrative techniques, for example in the way they present their characters. Whereas A 18 illustrated how physical descriptions can be used to explain personality, unit A 19 focusses on the technique of revealing personality through a person's behaviour and thoughts. Generally speaking, authors have two methods of presenting their characters. They either use the method of direct characterisation, that is they *tell* us about them, or the more indirect technique of *showing* us how they talk, think and act, leaving the reader to interpret their behaviour. The extract in task 1 illustrates the technique of direct characterisation, the one in task 4 that of indirect characterisation.
Besides becoming aware of narrative techniques, students are also encouraged to read creatively, imagining the characters and scenes described and thinking about how the story might develop.

1. Direct characterisation
Using an extract from a story by Roald Dahl students explore the narrative technique of direct characterisation. Because Dahl describes his character explicitly the readers do not have to draw too many conclusions for themselves. Students learn that if a fictional character is described in this direct manner they can use the author's own words in their interpretation.

Pick out words …
At this stage the class only pick out words from the text. (See table below.)

Mr Hazell's personality	Evidence
– rich beyond words	– his property stretched for miles … All the land around us belonged to him … the vast ocean of Mr Hazell's estate
– a roaring snob	– he tried desperately to get in with what he believed were the right kind of people … He hunted with the hounds … shooting parties … fancy waistcoats … silver Rolls-Royce
– drinking too much beer	– great glistening beery face … soft and inflamed

A 19 Teaching notes

Try to imagine ...
In a brainstorming session groups or pairs of students collect ideas about Mr Hazell, developing the character and imagining how he might behave in everyday situations and how he relates to those around him. Results are read out and discussed.

2. Use your imagination
A creative reading of the extract is further encouraged by asking the class to imagine the setting, the relationship between the three characters and to put forward hypotheses as to further developments.

Draw a map ...
Pairs or groups of learners draw rough sketches to indicate the relative extent of Mr Hazell's land compared with that of the narrator's father. Mr Hazell's land could feature his large brewery, should extend on both sides of a valley and should have a road going through the middle of it. Somewhere in the centre should be a small filling station. Students decide how to indicate the properties (e.g. by squares labelled 'B' for brewery and 'G' for garage) and also ownership of the land, e.g. by the letter 'H' for Hazell.

Can you imagine ...?
Working in groups or pairs the class make notes on the possible relationship between the characters in the extract. They will probably suggest that Mr Hazell will try to bully the story-teller's father and may even want to buy his land. They could speculate as to his methods and the father's reactions. The boy could take a passive role or could try to support his father by playing tricks on their enemy.

3. Me and my kind of people
The extract is a starting point for a personalisation exercise in which learners describe both themselves and the kind of people they like, either orally or in writing.

Are you like ...?
After silently reading the extract students are allowed a few minutes to jot down a few notes. They then describe themselves and the kind of people they like, either orally and/or in writing. Answers can be read out to the class or other members of the group.

4. Indirect characterisation
Whereas the extract in task 1 illustrated the literary technique of largely telling the reader what a character is like, here personality is revealed by the more indirect method of showing the character's thoughts and feelings. The readers are left to draw their own conclusions.

Explain ...
a) Terry is surprised at his own reactions, that he does not really mind his mother leaving. He feels guilty because he is not sorry about it. He is glad, though, that he will not have to experience his parents' fights any longer.
b) The writer shows us Terry's thoughts and lets us imagine what he is like (in contrast to the extract in task 1, in which the author explicitly told us what kind of person Mr Hazell was).
c) 'I'm alone ... The car': By breaking the chain of thoughts up into short phrases and putting each one on a separate line the writer helps us to imagine the gradual way Terry begins to understand the situation. The thoughts come to him one at a time.

What do you think ...?
Using the clues in the extract learners will probably deduce that the first thing Terry does is try to drive the car. They would have to decide whether he can drive or not. If he can, he could set off on a trip, alone or with friends, locally or further afield, perhaps even leaving home, too. If he cannot drive yet the story line could be that he has an accident and damages other people's cars or property.

What would you do?
Orally or in writing students try to put themselves in Terry's place.

A 20 Characterisation through dialogue/writing dialogue

In playscripts personality cannot be described directly as in fiction, but is revealed by what the characters say and the way they speak and behave. Besides analysing the characters in the scene of a play, students also become sensitised to style as an element of characterisation.

1. A conversation between two schoolgirls
The class reads the scene silently. They will probably have difficulty understanding some of the colloquial expressions, but should try to guess their meanings.

Are there any words you cannot guess?
The following expressions may be difficult to guess:
- the Helen Clarks an' them – people like Helen Clark who are good at sports/good runners
- stuck-up: big-headed, arrogant
- Hang on – wait a minute
- so rotten fast – so terribly / awfully fast
- I'm getting carried away (to get carried away) – to become enthusiastic
- We'll be carried off – to be taken away to hospital
- skiving off (to skive off) – to avoid something by staying away or leaving early
- nip in – to go somewhere for a short time
- tuck in – to join the rest
- a top-up (also a 'fill-up') – some more to drink, to fill a cup up
- Marathon – the name of the biscuits

2. Style
Attention is drawn to style as a literary technique, deliberately chosen by writers to achieve specific aims.

Look at ...
The girls use the colloquial language of everyday speech, e.g.:
- elision in rapid speech: 'an; short forms: Don't, It's etc.
- incomplete sentences: (It's) Not fair, miss; (I) Wouldn't cheer ...; (I) Don't want ...; (There's) Nowhere to put it.

The writer has chosen this style in order to make his characters seem realistic.

3. Dialogue reveals character
The difference between 'a character', meaning a figure in a fictional work, and 'personality', meaning personal qualities, should be pointed out.
Working in groups or pairs, students analyse the two characters from the clues in the scene and then try to develop them further. At the same time they revise adjectives for describing people.

Pick out ...
The girls are described, using the vocabulary suggested. Words can be used twice and others can be added. Answers will vary.
One suggestion:
<u>Claire</u>: adventurous, cheeky, dishonest, disobedient, domineering, egoistic, fun-loving, imaginative, impulsive, independent, lively, open, popular, self-confident, tough
<u>Paula</u>: cautious, conscientious, co-operative, hard-working, honest, obedient, peace-loving, polite, quiet, respectful, responsible, serious, slow to show feelings, timid, well-behaved

What do you ...?
Learners can try to visualise the two characters by drawing sketches. They should think about facial expression, hair-style and clothes.

4. What next?
Students exchange their ideas about what happens next and then write out the final scene. They can read out these scenes within the groups or perform them in front of the whole class.

A 21 Humour through taking things literally

An extract from the children's classic 'Alice in Wonderland' focusses attention on the humour resulting from utterances being taken literally. Students become further sensitised to this kind of humour by a collection of jokes based on literal meaning.

1. An unusual meeting
Students read the passage silently, guessing the meanings of any unknown words.

Suggest …
The capital letter suggests that the animal is a person.

What is …?
Alice is a polite, well-behaved girl, which she shows by wanting to address the Cat by name. Since she does not know its name she invents one. Her good manners are also illustrated by the way she asks for directions, 'Would you tell me, please …?'

2. Thinking about humour
Students analyse the source of the humour in the passage, namely that the Cat takes Alice's words literally, instead of giving her the conventional response she expects.

How do you think …?
Alice expected the Cat to reply in the conventional, polite manner. She thought it would say something like 'Certainly/Of course. Where do you want to go?'

Explain why …
Alice tries to be very polite, but the Cat takes her words literally. This is not only unexpected and funny, it also exposes what she says as empty phrases. It makes Alice think about the meaning of what she has said.

Can you see …?
The Cat's behaviour could be seen as a criticism of the careless, meaningless way language is used in polite conversation.

3. Who is mad?
Look at …
The Cat very wittily shows Alice that things can be looked at in different ways and that what is 'mad' to one person (or creature) is normal to another. Alice, probably unintentionally, supports this argument by disagreeing with the Cat's description of the sound it makes — to the Cat it is growling, whereas to her it is purring. This confirms the Cat's point that there are no fixed norms because they are all relative and subjective.

4. The Cat's point of view
Having been reminded that things can be seen from various different points of view students apply this insight by thinking about how the Cat might perceive Alice.

Imagine …
Learners work in groups or pairs and compare their suggestions.
Some ideas:
– *This child is stupid/strange/funny (=peculiar, not humourous)/…*
– *She seems to be a stranger round here/…*
– *She doesn't seem to know me/where she is/be normal/…*
– *She thinks in an odd way/I can help her in some way/I'm stupid*
– *She doesn't know how to think/talk/find her way about*
etc.

5. Taking things literally
Students become sensitised to the humour resulting from taking things literally by matching questions with unexpected, literal replies.

Can you …?
1D, 2F, 3E, 4G, 5A, 6B, 7C.

In groups …
Working in groups the class try to think of some unexpected responses of their own. The activity could also take the form of a competition between two teams. When they can no longer go on the answers can be provided, but in the wrong order. Learners then have the task of matching them up correctly.
Some suggestions:
1. How can you make so many mistakes in one day? – *I get up early.*
2. I've had to punish you every day this week, Brian. What have you got to say? – *I'm glad it's Friday.*
3. I asked you to write an essay on cheese last night. – *I tried, but the cheese kept blocking my biro.*
4. I hope I didn't see you looking at Susan's paper, Tony? – *So do I.*

5. If I had six apples and wanted to divide them between eight children, how would I do it? – *Make a cake.*
6. If your father knew how badly you've behaved, Johnny, he'd get grey hair overnight. – *He'd be pleased at that. He's bald.*
7. We start school at nine. – *That's all right. If I'm not here you can start without me.*
8. Which part of going to school do you like best? – *The holidays.*

A 22 Humorous poems: nonsense, puns/ writing poetry

Students are introduced to some typical expressions of British humour – nonsense verse (task 1) and puns or 'plays on words' (tasks 2 and 3). No European language lends itself to plays on words better than English and nowhere is punning taken to more extreme lengths than in Britain. The intellectual prestige attached to puns surprises Germans, who have been brought up to scorn them as rather stale jokes. It is only gradually that puns are beginning to be appreciated in Germany, too.
There are two types of puns, both illustrated in this unit:
1. Phonological puns (task 2) rely on words or phrases with different meanings, but which sound the same (homophones). These are typically found in auditory jokes.
2. Semantic puns play on the double meanings of a word or phrase (homonyms and polysemous words).

   A creative attitude to poetry and language is encouraged by asking learners to compose a whole poem of their own (task 1) and to complete one by supplying missing lines (task 4).

1. A nonsense poem
Students explain the illogical statements in the poem and then correct them. They then use the poem as a model for producing a similar one of their own.

Explain …
You can't
– say 'I went' and 'tomorrow'
– take a front seat at the back
– fall from the bottom to the top/upwards
– break a front bone in your back.

If you
– eat some chocolate you can't give it to anyone
– phone for a taxi you don't walk home.

Correct …
The poem can be corrected in several different ways. Some suggestions:
I'm going to the pictures tomorrow / I went to the pictures yesterday.
I took a front seat / I took a back seat.
I climbed from the pit to the gallery
I fell from the gallery to the pit
And broke a front bone (in my chest) / And broke a bone in my back.
A lady gave me some chocolate,
I ate it and thanked her / I didn't eat it, but gave it her back.
I phoned for a taxi and rode home
And that's why I never came back (unchanged).

In groups …
Groups or pairs of learners try to make up a similar poem.

2. Playing with words
The humour in this poem arises from the phonological play on the phrase 'up at eight o'clock', which, read at normal speed, sounds like 'a potato clock'.

Read this poem aloud …
The reader does not become aware of the meaning 'up at eight o'clock' until the last stanza and only then if the poem is read aloud. As they read, students also become aware of the element of rhythm in poetry.

3. Recognising puns
The humorous effect of this poem results from the semantic play on words.

Pick them out …
Working in pairs or groups learners try to pick out and explain the puns. They will probably need dictionaries.

A 22 Teaching notes

A 23

Double meanings (puns):
- *bed: the bottom of a river; a piece of furniture we sleep in*
- *head: the bit of a hammer you hit things with; part of the human body*
- *foot: the bottom of a mountain; part of the leg*
- *hose: pair of trousers; garden equipment*
- *eye: the hole in a needle; part of the face*
- *wing: side section of a building; part of a butterfly*
- *ribs: bones in the chest; the metal rods of a parasol or umbrella*
- *trunk: bottom part of a tree; large case*
- *teeth: part of a rake; part of the mouth used for biting*
- *hands: part of a clock; on the end of the arm*
- *plot: piece of land; secret plan*
- *bark: the outer layer of a tree trunk; the sound a dog makes*

4. Writing your own poem
Working in groups or pairs learners fill in the gaps with excuses for not doing homework. Since the poem is in free verse the lines do not need to rhyme.

How many excuses …?
The class read out their poems to each other and then compare them with the original:

> **Where's your homework?**
>
> Smith! Where's your homework?
> *The dog ate it,* Sir.
> Oh, ok do it again then.
>
> Poulter! Where's your homework?
> *It just burst into flames,* Sir.
> Oh, ok do it again then.
>
> Rudd! Where's your homework?
> *It was stolen by aliens,* Sir.
> Oh, ok do it again then.
>
> Rendell! Where's your homework?
> Here it is, Sir.
> But this is a blank sheet of paper!
> *It's in invisible ink,* Sir.
> Oh, ok good lad.

> Sexton! Where's your homework?
> I haven't done it, Sir.
> Why haven't you done it?
> Because I watched T.V. instead, Sir.
> Do you expect me to believe
> Such a stupid excuse, boy?

A 23 Irony and euphemisms in a fable

James Thurber's fable *The rabbits who caused all the trouble* is used to give students the following insights:
1. Humour can be created by irony (tasks 1, 3).
2. Language can be misused in order to hide the truth (task 2).
3. The function of scapegoats in a literary text and in society generally (tasks 4, 5).
4. The typical features of a fable (tasks 6, 7).

1. A fable
The fable is read silently, any new words being guessed at.

List the reasons … How do you …?
1. The wolves said they did not like the rabbits' way of life.
   The readers will be amazed that the narrator agrees with the wolves' arrogant statement that their way of life is 'the only way to live'. They will begin to distrust the narrator's judgement and see that they must rely on their own opinions.
2. The wolves said that the rabbits caused an earthquake in which some wolves were killed.
   This comment is presented as a simple statement of facts. But it is so absurd that readers can only interpret it ironically. They will want to find out what the narrator really means.
3. The wolves blamed the rabbits for the lightning which killed one wolf.
   This comment reinforces the readers' conviction that the narrator is being ironic and is really ridiculing the wolves by exposing their hypocrisy.
4. The wolves accused the rabbits of causing a flood which drowned many of the wolves.
   Like the preceding comment, this one confirms

the readers' opinion that the story is an ironic attack on the wolves.

Do you see …?
It now becomes clear that the title is meant ironically, exposing the incongruity between what the reader expects and what actually happens.

2. Misusing language to disguise the truth
The fable exposes the way those in power frequently misuse language to mislead others and further their own interests.

Give examples …
Through the Looking Glass (1871) is the sequel to Lewis Carroll's famous *Alice in Wonderland* (1865). The quotation illustrates the way the wolves distort language in order to exercise power over others:

– *The wolves 'threatened to civilize the rabbits if they didn't behave'. The word 'civilise' sounds harmless, but disguises its real meaning, implied by the word 'threatened'. 'Civilise' here is a euphemism, an expression which is intended to make the real meaning of a word sound more acceptable. The wolves probably intend to kill and eat the rabbits.*
  The verb 'civilise' is a reminder of the colonial period of the eighteenth and nineteenth centuries when western powers tried to justify their aggression against other countries by explaining that they were 'civilising' them. Like the wolves, they imposed their own 'progressive' way of life on weaker peoples and tried to force them to 'behave'. A more modern example of such euphemisms is 'ethnic cleansing'.
– *Another example of how the wolves misuse language for their own purposes is the explanation they give for imprisoning the rabbits – it is 'for their own good … for their own protection'.*
– *The wolves' justification of their killing of the rabbits is a further illustration of how they distort language. They cynically twist the other animals' phrase, 'this is no world for escapists', to mean exactly the opposite. Instead of being an attempt to console the rabbits, coming from the wolves it becomes their death warrant. For if there is no place for escapists in the world it follows that they must be destroyed.*

Rephrase …
1. The American pioneers 'civilised' the natives – *they imposed their own way of life on them, made them subservient and even murdered them*
2. 'ethnic cleansing' – *killing certain ethnic groups of people or forcing them to leave their homes*
3. to 'liquidate' someone – *to kill someone*
4. to 'correct' borders – *to force some people to leave their homes and possibly kill some of them*
5. the soldiers 'took out' the rebels – *they killed them*
6. 're-education centres' – *prison camps where people are often tortured to make them 'change their minds'*
7. to 'rationalise' the organisation of a business – *to sack some workers*
8. 'adjustment to the work force' – *the sacking of workers*
9. 'an opportunity for a change of career' – *the sacking of workers*
10. a 'very physical' football player – *one who fouls a lot*

Students can try to think of further examples of euphemisms.

3. Irony
The powerful effect of the story is due to irony: firstly, the ironic contrast beween the wolves' words and deeds and, secondly, the contrast between the narrative style and the events described.

Explain …
The ironical effect of the story is reinforced by the contrast between the wolves' absurd accusations and the way the narrator presents them. The repeated comments 'it is well known that …' suggest that the wolves' statements are perfectly normal and universally accepted. This contrast between the events and the way they are described shocks and provokes the readers.

4. The rabbits as scapegoats
The wolves' creation of scapegoats is examined, also the general function of scapegoats in a society.

Explain ...
The wolves suggest that the rabbits are not normal because they behave differently from themselves (pound on the ground with their hind legs, eat lettuce and carrots). In the wolves' eyes these differences make them dangerous (they cause natural catastrophes).

Suggest ...
Scapegoats can be blamed for anything which goes wrong. This discourages people from thinking about who should really be blamed and directs aggression away from the real target. Scapegoats are chosen because they are too weak to fight back and also sufficiently 'different' to provide an outlet for pent-up aggression.

Students could exchange ideas on how to behave if they were treated as scapegoats or experienced someone else suffering from such treatment. They could form groups and make up short scenes in which one person or group is victimised in this way.

5. The other animals
In a role playing exercise the question of why the other animals did not help the rabbits is examined. The wolves seem to be the leaders and it is possible that the others were afraid of them. However, this is unlikely because the others demanded an explanation and the wolves felt obliged to give one. Most probably the others simply did not care what happened to the rabbits.
Pairs of learners can read out their dialogues to the rest of the class.

6. The allegory
Fables are allegorical, containing hidden comments, usually criticisms, of human behaviour. The characters, which are mostly animals, are stereotyped figures intended to represent certain types of human beings.

Decide ...
The characters symbolise the following groups in human society:
– The wolves: *the leaders/those in power*
– The rabbits: *the weakest, least powerful group in a society, those who can be used as scapegoats*
– The other animals: *the uncritical masses.*

Which of the animals ...? Translate ...
The wolves are attacked for their cruelty and hypocrisy. But it could be argued that the other animals are just as bad, if not worse. They are cowardly, indifferent and unreliable. Instead of protesting at the wolves hypocrisy and injustice they try to hide behind empty words. It is these others who are the escapists, not the rabbits. The warning to the readers is that they should not ignore injustice, but should protest and help those who are suffering.

Do you see ...?
Apart from the play on the word 'internal' (the rabbits are now inside the wolves), the wolves' statement reminds us of the warnings sometimes given by other nations not to interfere in their affairs. The class could discuss the conditions which might justify such intervention, for instance wars, crimes against human rights, discrimination against and maltreatment of minorities and women.

7. The moral
Pairs or groups of students try to think up their own moral for Thurber's fable and then compare their results with the author's.

Make up a ...
Some suggestions:
Do not blindly rely on others for help. With friends like that, who needs enemies? Do not let yourself be 'civilised'. It is nothing to do with me. Never interfere. Mind your own business? etc.

Further exercise
Using Thurber's tale as a model the class write their own fable. Generally, they follow Thurber's story line, but are given increasing freedom towards the end to introduce some variation, for instance the other animals' threat to the wolves and the justification given by the wolves. Results can be read out and compared.

Background information

Whilst Thurber's fable has a general relevance, the time when it was published, August 26, 1939 *(The New Yorker)* leads to the conclusion that there are some quite specific historical references. Fascism was becoming a real threat and Thurber felt the need to protest against the Nazis' treatment of Jews. It can be inferred that the rabbits represent the Jews and the wolves the Nazis. The other animals can be seen as symbols of the 'Free World', which refused to become involved. Despite vague promises of help to the German Jews, they would not take them in as refugees, even in America. At the 1938 world conference in Evian, summoned by the American president Roosevelt, all the participating countries stated that they could not accommodate large numbers of Jewish emigrants. Astonishingly, some European states such as Poland even tried to get rid of their own Jews. Against this background the slogan 'this is no world for escapists' appears in a new light, implying the widespread reluctance to accept rabbits (Jews) as escapists (refugees). Hence the rather selfish advice to the rabbits to stay and be brave. Later the wolves twist this slogan to justify their extermination of the escapists. The other animals must take a share of the blame for the rabbits' fate because they refused to acknowledge the injustice done to them and to offer them refuge in their own countries.

A 24 Writing the ending to a short story/ changing the point of view

A short story by Ronald Duncan (1914–1982), *When we dead awaken*, provides the opportunity for reading actively and creatively.

At the first reading the last few paragraphs are withheld and students make up their own endings. When presented with the original conclusion they realise that the narrator is a ghost. The impact of this unusual angle makes them aware of point of view as a narrative technique. The effect of the choice of narrator is underlined by contrast, as learners retell the story from a less dramatic point of view, that of the ghost's wife. A closer reading of the original reveals certain clues as to what happened, which brings home the advantages of reading in an active, alert way.

1. Interpreting a short story
Read this story …
The story is cut off at line 80, as indicated. Students read ls.1–80 silently and speculate about further developments. Working in groups or pairs they can note down a few ideas before writing their own endings. Selected endings are then read out.

2. The ending
Silently, the class read the original ending.

Compare …
The main difference between the original ending and the students' work will probably be that the learners' narrators are living people. They should realise that point of view is a narrative technique and that writers think very carefully about who is to tell their stories in order to achieve certain effects. Students may be able to give examples from their own reading of unusual points of view or of stories in which events are coloured by being presented through the eyes of a certain person.

3. Clues
Students are encouraged to take an active role in the reading process by looking for the clues as to what probably happened. Knowing the ending throws a different light on the previous events. Hints that the man fell and was killed are:
– *my eyes lost their fixed objective, I hesitated … (l. 66).*
– *later I found myself sitting on the beach; I do not know how long I had sat there … I do not know. (ls. 67–69).*
– *When the man returns he is surprised that there is a fire in the house. This suggests he has been away a long time because he left in May, a time when they hardly ever had a fire.*

4. Changing the point of view
The surprising impact of the unusual point of view is underlined by contrast with a less dramatic one, that of the ghost's wife. Working in pairs or groups the class first exchange ideas together before writing their own version.

Index of text types and reading and writing skills

Type of text   **Unit**

Type of text	Unit
Various text types	A1, A2
Commercial advertisements	A3, A6, A9
Travel guide	A4
Book descriptions ('blurbs')	A5
Encyclopedia article	A7
Informal letter	A8
Formal letter	A9
Magazine articles	A10, A13, A14, A16
Instructions	A11
Newspaper article	A12
Poem	A15
Science fiction extract	A17
Extracts from various literary texts	A18, A19, A20, A21
Humorous poems: puns	A22
Fable	A23
Short story	A24

Reading skills

Skill	Unit
Recognising different types of texts	A1, A2
Skimming advertisements	A3
Skimming to get a general idea of the text	A4
Skimming book descriptions ('blurbs')	A5
Scanning for specific information	A6, A7
Recognising informal and formal style in letters	A8, A9
Recognising the main points in a text	A4, A10, A12, A14, A16
Analysing an instructional text	A11
Analysing an argumentative text	A13
Creative reading	A15, A21, A24
Analysing descriptive techniques in literature	A18, A19, A20
Understanding humour through taking things literally	A21
Understanding puns	A22
Understanding irony	A23
Analysing point of view	A24

Writing skills

Skill	Unit
Making notes	A4, A7, A14, A16
Writing book descriptions ('blurbs')	A5
Explaining (sports) rules	A6
Writing informal letters	A8
Writing formal letters	A9
Reorganising information	A10
Writing instructions	A11
Linking ideas	A12, A16
Presenting arguments	A13, A14, A15
Writing a poem	A15, A22
Summarising non-fiction	A14, A16
Summarising fiction	A17
Describing physical appearance	A18
Describing personality	A19
Writing a drama scene	A20
Explaining a fable	A23
Writing the ending to a story / changing the point of view	A24